The 7-Step Lease Option Refinance Strategy

How to Profit in Real Estate with Minimal Risk

David Hamilton, M.Sc.

Copyright © 2014 David Hamilton

www.HootInvest.com

www.cardinalhomeinvestments.com

All rights reserved. No part of this publication may be reproduced or transmitted in any form or by any means, electronic or mechanical, including photocopying, recording, or any information storage and retrieval system, without permission in writing from the author.

ISBN-13: 978-1494767044

ISBN-10: 149476704X

Dedication

This book is dedicated to all honest, hard-working people who want to take more control of their financial futures by learning to invest themselves. Through the 7-Step Lease Option Refinance Strategy, not only will you learn to invest in real estate wisely, but you will also be helping other hard-working families keep their homes.

Contents

	Acknowledgments	vii
	Foreword: It Was a Dark and Stormy Night, or, How I Came to Write This Book	ix
1	Is Real Estate Still a Good Investment?	1
2	How This Strategy Can Generate Wealth the Low-Risk Way	7
3	What is a Real Estate Lease Option, and How Does it Work?	19
4	The 7-Step Lease Option Refinance Strategy	25
4.1	Step 1 – Identify Your Investment Funds	27
4.2	Step 2 – Select Your Team of Experts	35
4.3	Step 3 – Find a Qualified Property	45
4.4	Step 4 – Purchase the Property	61
4.5	Step 5 – Manage the Property	85
4.6	Step 6 – Sell the Property	95
4.7	Step 7 – Do it Again!	99
5	A Typical Refinance Scenario: Making the Strategy Work in the Real World	103
6	Turbocharge Your Wealth Through Lease Option Refinancing	111

7	When Your Investment Goes Horribly Wrong	115
8	How to Make Lease Option Refinancing Work With No Money of Your Own	125
9	Frequently Asked Questions on Lease Option Refinancing	133
10	The Cardinal Home Investments Refinance Program For Investors	139
11	Glossary of Terms	141
12	Appendices	145

Acknowledgements

I would like to thank first and foremost my business partners Rob Cornforth and Sean Lynch from Cardinal Home Investments. I would also like to thank my team of real estate professionals for helping me along the way: Sherri Clark at Sherri's Bookkeeping Services, Frank Falsetto at Hamilton-Appotive, Steve Ernst at Converge Financial, George Dube at Dube and Cuttini, April Stewart at Landlord Legal, mortgage broker Rose Vitagliano, and Patrick Caicco at Altaview Financial.

Investors should be aware that there are no guarantees in real estate investing, and using the strategy outlined here could make or lose you money. Real estate investing is not for everyone. Please conduct your own analyses carefully and consult with your accountant or lawyer prior to investing.

Foreword:
It Was a Dark and Stormy Night, or, How I Came To Write This Book

It really was a dark and stormy night. It was also in the dead of a cold, snowy Canadian winter when I realized that I had to do something about getting my finances together. I was by myself in my home – the rest of the family was fast asleep – and I was worrying about my health and my retirement and what I might be able to do to make a living. You see, I had just finished six months of chemotherapy after going through surgery to have a 4 inch cancerous tumor removed from my gut. Just before that, as luck would have it, I had left my career in government to forge out on my own as a real estate investor and part-time teacher. And now I wasn't sure how my health would hold out, never mind how I was going to build a business when my energy levels were so low.

It was, indeed, a dark and stormy night for sure.

With that as the backdrop, I needed to find a way to make sure my family would be taken of financially if something ever happened to me again. I wanted to be able to send my son to any university he

Foreword

wanted to go, and I wanted to make sure my wife would be able to retire in comfort. The question for me was: how to do this with limited available time and energy?

As I gained experience in real estate, I soon learned that it was really easy to spend a lot of money in numerous high-risk investments. I was really attracted to the potential returns available in real estate, but I sure didn't like the risk associated with those returns. So I needed to find a way to enjoy solid returns without taking on too much risk, and without having to wait 20 years or so for the market to build up my equity.

What I researched and found was the concept of using lease options to help homeowners refinance their homes. I came across this idea through an investigation of various rent to own schemes which, frankly, I didn't feel all that comfortable with. And the way lease options were being used to help some people refinance their homes was also risky, but I saw the potential in it if a solid, low-risk approach was used with it.

Thus, the idea for the 7-Step Lease Option Refinance Strategy was born. Over the past several years, this strategy has evolved to the point now where I feel extremely confident and comfortable that it can work for just about any investor, anywhere in the world. The low-risk principles have been tested in real world transactions and have proven to be excellent. So risk is minimized and yet returns still average over 20% per year. That's not bragging or embellishing. That's fact.

And I'm not the only investor who has been achieving those returns with this strategy. Not only do I invest with the 7-Steps, but my colleagues and I also help other investors do the same. Now, when I reflect back on the dark and stormy nights from before, I do so with the realization that I have been so completely blessed in this world, and that I'm thrilled to be able to pay my gratitude forward to other investors.

David Hamilton
Ottawa, Ontario

Chapter 1

Is Real Estate Still a Good Investment?

Kindness is always fashionable.

Amelia Barr

If you're looking at this book in a book store – either a virtual one or a physical one – you know there are many books written about making money in real estate. Some are good and some are nothing more than motivational "make your list of dreams" with promises of no money down riches, beaches, babes, cool drinks and fast cars. But do regular people actually make real money from these things?

I can tell you that in my experience, no one has made the kind of money these self-appointed gurus talk about in the short time they promise.

No. One.

In fact, thousands of people have *lost* significant amounts of money by falling into some of these get rich quick schemes. They borrow money from credit cards for down payments, throw any old tenant in the home, and then run into trouble and don't know what to do about it.

That doesn't mean that a regular person with average intelligence can't do well investing in real estate. You can! But in my experience, there is no such thing as getting rich quick in any business, and real estate is no exception. It simply does not happen. And before someone writes me to tell me about Uncle George who bought a distress sale home and flipped it for a fortune, let me qualify my statement by saying, okay, it *can* happen. Just like people *can* win lotteries and get hit by lightning. It *can* happen. But these situations are so rare that for the vast majority of us, it's nothing more than wishful thinking.

Listen. I'm here to tell you that you can make money in real estate. But I'm also going to tell you the truth: it won't happen over night. If you're looking for a get rich quick book, this is not it.

So here's what I know about really making money in real estate. The following strategies do not involve flipping or anything like that, and none of them are short-term deals.

Being a Buy Low, Sell High Vulture

The first is the "buy low and sell high" property. This is one you'll hear about a lot on late night television these days, or when the latest guru sweeps into town. In this case, you as the investor keep your eyes open for a home that is either in foreclosure or about to go into foreclosure. Then you make a ridiculously low offer to the homeowners who feel compelled to accept it because they are in such financial straits. Once you buy the home at a crazy low price, you can then put in some fresh paint and carpeting, and rent it out or sell it again. Most choose to rent it out.

Without question, this can work. But of course, you need to select the property very carefully to make sure you're not getting a dump. And then you need to know the real estate market really well in that neighbourhood to ensure you're getting a good deal. And then you either need to find the right tenants – which makes this investment as hands on as you can get – or else you need to be able to turn the house around and sell it. This presumes that you have sufficient financing to carry the costs of the mortgage, insurance, property taxes, upkeep etc., while the house is on the market.

So this way – buying low and selling at a profit – is certainly a viable way to make money in real estate if you're looking for a hands-on investment and you have sufficient funds at hand. However, it requires specialized knowledge and sufficient funds to draw on.

Buying and Renting a Condo Apartment

Another way to make money in real estate is to get into the condo market. In most major cities in North America, condo apartment buildings continue to be extremely popular, and the boom in these homes has certainly been felt. However, there is considerable risk associated with many of these condos. Let's go through a few of them now so you know what you're getting into if you go this route.

First, chances are you have to put money down on a condo that hasn't even been built yet. There's no guarantee that it will ever get built and I suspect you may already know some investors who put down deposits on condos and then never saw their money again.

Second, when you buy a new condo, you're actually being a real estate *speculator*. You are gambling that the demand for condo housing is greater than the number of available units. That way, you can charge high rents, cover your costs, and eventually sell your condo down the road for additional profit.

Third, and perhaps this is the greatest risk, unless you sit on the condo board of directors, decisions will be made that can have a significant impact on your monthly cash flow. For example, the board may need cash to fix windows or elevators or roofs. Or do landscaping. Or put in a new pool. Or… the list goes on and on. As an investor, you need to be really clear on your monthly expenses to make sure that whatever revenues you get from tenants will cover your costs. If you choose to invest in a condo, you will never have cost certainty. That's why I don't invest in condos and will have nothing to do with them as an investor. More on that later!

Finally, you never know when the condo market will disappear. There are so many buildings going up these days in all major cities that at some point, the supply will outstrip the demand. When that happens, you may be stuck with an overvalued condo and no tenants with hardly any on the horizon. That spells an investment disaster.

Long-Term Buy and Hold

Let's now look at the traditional, long-term way that most investors make money in real estate: the buy and hold strategy.

In this strategy, you find a decent single-family home in a growing neighbourhood, purchase it at a reasonably good price, and then rent it out for several years to well-selected tenants. This is, in fact, the way that true real estate riches are made. Even if the economy isn't great, your rental income will cover your expenses and your tenants slowly pay off your mortgage. When times are good, you can make a lot of money through market appreciation.

I use this strategy for some of my properties. I have a few that are long-term rentals and I plan to hold on to them for 20 years or more. I won't get rich quickly from them, but as long as they are well-managed and in good shape, I should be able to use them for my future retirement

And that, my friends, is the key: these are long-term investments and they are also hands on investments. If you have tenants, then you can expect to get calls at any time of the day or night about every little thing that needs to get done. Plugged toilets. Garage door openers that don't work. Carpeting that needs replacing. A window that won't open properly. A fence that needs mending. Roof shingles. Snow removal. Wells running dry. Furnaces breaking down. Broken branches. Wasp nests and mice infestations (yep, I've even had these!). Grass cutting… the list goes on and on.

If you're lucky, you'll find long-term tenants who take care of many of these things themselves, but don't count on it. Alternatively, you can find yourself a good property manager to handle all those day to day annoyances, but remember, you will pay for this service so again, being clear on your monthly expenses is really important.

Other Real Estate Investments

How else can you make money in real estate? Well there are other investment vehicles like real estate investment funds and trusts. You can also invest in second mortgages too. These are both more sophisticated ways to make money, and they both carry their own share of risks. With real estate funds, you don't control your money and the management fees can eat you up if you're not careful. With second mortgages, you need to do a lot of due diligence and they carry a certain amount of risk too. If there's ever a problem and the property goes into foreclosure, because your mortgage is in second place behind the first mortgage lender – usually a bank – then you may lose a significant amount of your cash.

When I started investing in real estate, I tried to learn as much as I could about everything. It was overwhelming. I have invested in condos (never again!), long-term rentals, investment trusts, second mortgages, and rent to own schemes. I have made money with some and lost money with others. And throughout my experience, I have been able to put together a strategy that not only works, but carries minimal risk and is virtually 100% hands free once you've set it up. It's the subject of this book: my 7-Step Lease Option Refinance Strategy. And I will show you how you can take your own cash (or partner up with someone who has the funds if you don't), and put together a plan for making about a million dollars profit in about a dozen years. It is based on my years of experience as an investor, landlord, and business modeler. And, I can tell you that I have yet to find anything else out there that will produce the kind of outstanding returns (about 25% per year) with the solid risk mitigation that this strategy does.

I can't wait to share it with you!

Chapter Highlights

- There are many ways to make money in real estate, and many ways to lose a lot of money in real estate! Be sure to choose an investment vehicle that suits you.
- The 7-Step Lease Option Refinance Strategy is one of the few investment strategies that minimizes all major risks in real estate. While there are no guarantees in investing or in life, this strategy is definitely a lower-risk vehicle than many others out there.

Chapter 2

How This Strategy Can Generate Wealth the Low-Risk Way

I've failed over and over and over again in my life and that is why I succeed.

Michael Jordan

So you can probably tell by now that I don't mess around with a lot of fluff and mush. This is not a "feel good" book about goal-setting and being all you can be or finding your inner child or anything like that. This is a book about a real estate investment strategy that consistently works anywhere, and how you can use it to build your own wealth without a lot of hands-on work and without taking on a lot of risk. It's about making money, yes, and just as importantly, it's also about not losing money!

What I've Learned

Before we get into the nuts and bolts of this strategy – and why it's a better real estate investment strategy than most you'll come across these days – I want to take a few minutes to tell you about my own experience and why I'm putting my strategy into a book and sharing it with thousands of investors like you. First, let me assure you that I have made just about every mistake a novice real estate investor can make. I've purchased absolute dumps and – here's a surprise – lost a ton of money on them with bad tenants and crazy repair bills. I've had tenants come into my homes and then never pay their rent on time. I've had houses sit empty because the tenants have moved out and the market values dipped. I've had so-called professional property managers treat my properties and my tenants poorly, so again, I end up losing money. I've joined real estate investment clubs that are filled with sharks and wanna-be investors who talk big but don't actually do anything except try to separate me from my investment money.

These are not happy experiences, let me assure you. After being drawn into the possibility of making a fortune in real estate, my early experiences have been the exact opposite. I have lost money. I have gone into so much debt that some days I wondered what I was going to do. I've had many a sleepless night wondering how I would pay my mortgages. But, fortunately, it doesn't have to be this way for you.

I am an optimist. I do believe there are ways to make excellent returns on real estate without taking on a ton of risk and without having to deal with crappy tenants and broken water pipes (yes, I've had those too) and so on. I believe we live in a world of abundance, and I believe that what goes around, comes around. The universe has a way of rewarding and punishing, and it can never be fooled.

The key, of course, was discovering the right strategy that would work for someone like me… someone who wants to do well in real estate investing in the long-term, and who doesn't want to do a lot of grunt work, and who understands that real estate investing is not a get rich quick proposition. Something like…

The 7-Step Lease Option Strategy Unmasked

In this chapter, I'm going to give you the general overview of what the 7-Step Lease Option Refinance Strategy is, and how it can work for you.

At the most basic level, you are going to work with experienced mortgage brokers to find a family living in a single-family home that has run into financial trouble and is in danger of losing their home to the bank. You will perform your due diligence on the family's financial history (I'll show you how) and if it all checks out, you will purchase their home from them. By liberating the equity in their home, they will be able to pay off most if not all of their consumer debts.

Then, you will lease it back to them for a three year period while they get their financial house in order. This means they don't have to move. You will also give them the first right of refusal when you sell it. For this opportunity, they will give you a non-refundable "option to purchase" as consideration for this chance to buy it back first. The option to purchase comprises 12 months of expenses and is held in trust by your lawyer.

Each month, the family will pay you a monthly occupancy payment (rent). You pay the mortgage, property taxes, insurance, property management, and you pay yourself a healthy return.

At the end of three years, the family will secure a new mortgage and use their option to purchase as the down payment when they buy the house back from you. When their purchase closes, you take your proceeds and find another family to help out.

See, the thing about this investment strategy is that not only are you going to make considerable money with minimal risk, but you are also helping a family keep their home. No one wants to go through the humiliating experience of having to sell the family home, pull the kids out of school and move to a rental because they can't get a new mortgage. With this strategy, the family stays in their home while they work with credit professionals to get their finances re-established.

The original homeowner—who then becomes your tenant—depends on you to help them out of their financial bind. They have equity in their home, sure, but they cannot get access to it because for whatever reason, their credit is no good. No lender will therefore give them a home equity loan. I have found that a typical homeowner who comes to us runs into this catch-22. They may lose their job for a few months, live off their credit cards, not pay their mortgage, and then when their mortgage comes up for renewal, the bank won't do it. What's worse, if the homeowner goes to a mortgage broker to find someone else to give them a mortgage, those other lenders won't do it either because of their poor credit rating.

This leaves the homeowner with very few options. They can either sell their home and move into a rental. Or they can try to get a mortgage from a private lender (very expensive). Or they can come to you, who will not only give them a decent, affordable monthly payment, but will also allow them to free up the equity in their home so they can pay down their debts and get a fresh start. The private lenders cannot compete with that.

At this point, you may be wondering if this strategy is too complicated for you, or if there really are people out their who will sell their homes to you. What I can tell you from my experience is that there are a lot of families in precarious financial positions right now and they are desperate to find a solution so they can keep their homes. I can also tell you that nothing about this strategy is complicated or overly-demanding for most people; however, there is a lot of work to do up front… I won't lie to you about that. Once you've done that upfront work, though, the rest of it is pretty simple. And besides, you won't be doing this alone. You will have a team of real estate professionals working with you—from brokers, to lawyers, and property managers. And there are companies like Cardinal Home Investments who are available for consultations and helping you manage the entire process if you so wish. So you will have support at each step of the way.

Assumptions

Before we go into the strategy step by step, I want to outline some basic assumptions about this exciting way to make money in real estate without taking on too many risks. As we go through these assumptions, please don't worry if some of them don't apply to you. Investors come in all shapes and sizes. Some have lots of working capital, others don't. Some have their investment funds tied up in government-sponsored "registered" savings or retirement plans. Some partner up with others and go in as a team. The point of this section is simply to outline what some of the basic assumptions are, and if you need to modify some of them to fit your own particular circumstances, that's fine.

1. **You have $100k to invest**

I will tell you right now that this, by far, is the most difficult part of the entire strategy. And not only for the 7-Step Lease Option Refinance Strategy but also for any kind of real estate investment. You will need cash and you will need a tidy sum of it. Or, you will need *access* to this cash.

There are several ways of pulling this investment money together if you don't happen to have it sitting in your bank account. The easiest, simplest way to find the cash is to pull it out of your own home, and that leads us to the next assumption.

2. **You own your home (and have equity in it)**

You get your investment cash from a home equity loan, which assumes of course that you own your own home, and have sufficient equity in it so that you can put in place a home equity loan and borrow the funds from it to invest. It also assumes that you can service the loan, so you need to have regular income in order to qualify for it.

There are a couple of reasons why you'll want to use the equity in your own home for investment purposes. The first is, right now in 2014, the interest rates on home equity loans are very low… typically around 3 – 4% as I'm writing. As such, the cost of borrowing this money is minimal. Moreover, when you borrow money to invest, you are eligible to write off many of the expenses associated with borrowing the money against income from the investment itself. In other words, if you pay $100 a month in interest on your home equity loan, and you've used that loan to invest in real estate that brings in $200 a month in revenues, you can use that loan interest to offset the gains in your revenue, thereby reducing your taxable income. That's a huge tax win!

Each investor's situation is unique, so you will naturally want to discuss all this with your accountant so that you understand exactly what the tax implications are—and how you can minimize your tax situation—before you start investing. This actually rings true no matter what kind of real estate investment you plan to make. As I have learned, real estate professionals like knowledgeable accountants and lawyers can be your best friends.

If you are not a homeowner and do not have equity to draw from, fear not! There are other ways to find investment money even if you don't have your own cash or assets. We'll cover all those in Chapter 8.

3. You can secure your own first mortgage

This may seem a bit obvious, but banks these days are totally unpredictable when it comes to securing a new first mortgage on an income property. When I began investing several years ago, banks would give mortgages to anyone with a decent job and a pulse. They only required a 5% down payment and you were on your way. They also told me that if I wanted unlimited first mortgages, all I needed to do was put 65% down on a home, and I could have hundreds of mortgages.

Well, if you've been following the mortgage and lending trends for the past couple of years, you know this has changed completely. Banks are now extremely stingy and the requirements you need to meet in order to secure a new first mortgage are frustrating and numerous.

There are things you can do to better prepare for your discussion about mortgages. This is where an experienced mortgage broker can really help out. We'll cover all that shortly.

So, now we have access to $100k and we're going to get that from a home equity loan if we don't have the cash sitting in the bank. And we also feel that we have sufficient ability to secure our own first mortgage on an income property. So far, so good. The next assumption we're going to make is...

4. You only invest in economically stable areas

Believe me, the worst thing you could do is invest your hard-earned cash in a town or region that is losing jobs. Under this strategy, we need property to at least hold its value over the next three years. I'll show you that you could, indeed, withstand a bit of a decrease in property values if needed, but since we have a choice as to where we can invest, it only makes sense to put our money into property that's in a growing area in order to minimize the risk of losing any of our investment.

This reminds me again of what this strategy is all about, so I'll remind you again of it too. Yes, this is a strategy designed to earn you considerable money over time. But just as important, this strategy is also designed to minimize the risk of losing your money!

There are no guarantees in real estate investing of course, so the next best thing we can do is look at all the possible risks—all those things that could go horribly wrong—and put measures in place to reduce the possibility of them happening. The 7-Step Lease Option Refinance Strategy—at least the way I do it—accomplishes this.

Suppose you live in an area of the country that isn't doing well economically, so investing in your own region is problematic. Well a couple of things can happen. First, even in declining communities, there are still neighbourhoods that are desirable and in demand. You would need to focus on them. The challenge here is that the risk is still greater than if you were to invest in an economically growing area. And, you may not find the right homeowner clients. The second thing you could do—and one that I would recommend—is to work with a mortgage broker to find a good community and solid homeowner-clients somewhere else in the country. There's nothing stopping you from investing outside your own neighbourhood, but there are things you need to do, steps you need to take, to ensure that you don't run into a whole other set of problems trying to manage a property that is half-way across the nation. Not to worry, I've done this, and I'll show you what you need to do.

5. You will only invest in single-family homes and never in condominiums

The best type of property to invest in is a fully detached single-family home. Duplexes and townhomes are okay, but if you share a roof with someone, be prepared to share expenses when something goes wrong. If possible—and believe me, it is possible—avoid purchasing anything other than a fully detached, non-condominium, single-family home.

So you may be wondering why I don't like condos. Well the problem with condos is that you cannot control your investment. The condo association and its board of directors controls these things. So if they need more money for the reserve fund, they will take it from you (not the tenant). If the roof needs replacing or something else goes horribly wrong, you will need to pay for it along with the other homeowners in the development. And, more and more what we're seeing these days is condo fees that are almost as expensive as mortgages. It's crazy!

Do yourself a favour and avoid all kinds of headaches and just say no to condos. Make that promise to yourself, and you'll save yourself a ton of problems. How do I know? Because I've lived through these experiences and I can tell you that I have never had a good experience with a condo. Ever. Yes, I know they are sexy and "everybody is doing it", but for me, earning money in a low-risk investment is way sexier. Way.

6. You will always secure at least 12 months of expenses as security

Your biggest risk in the 7-Step Lease Option Refinance Strategy is if the tenants decide to bail out and just take off, leaving you with all kinds of expenses and no income. Conventional wisdom says to hold back at least three months of property expenses (mortgage, taxes, insurance etc.) in a reserve fund in case of this emergency. But I have found that three months is not nearly enough. In fact, six months may not even be enough. And what's worse, if the tenants decide not to pay their rent and you have to go through an eviction process, that process could take months and months before it gets resolved, depending on where the property is and whether the local landlord-tenant board understands what a lease option is.

Without question, dealing with tenants is the biggest headache in this or in any other real estate investment strategy that depends on rental income.

One of the benefits of having the previous homeowners become tenants in their old home is that they tend to take care of it better than other tenants who just walk in off the street. They still see it as their home, and because they plan to buy it back in a few years, they will want to look after it. Moreover, the occupancy agreement you sign with them (we'll cover this in Chapter 4: Step 4) stipulates that they—not you—are responsible for things like plugged toilets, furnace repairs, snow removal, and so on. In other words, their responsibilities for these things do not change under this strategy, even though ownership of the property has.

But the point about the expenses is this: you will need at least 12 months of expenses held in reserve in case the tenant misses a monthly payment, takes off, or needs to be evicted. So the assumption here is that you will not accept any deal where there is less than 12 months of expenses available as an option to purchase. If you can get more, then that's even better.

These funds do not come from your pocket. They come from the tenants' equity in their home, so when you're selecting a homeowner to help, this is a critical point. They must have sufficient equity to pay down their consumer debts, pay you your up front fee (oh yes, your efforts up front are rewarded), and put at least 12 months of expenses into the option to purchase for security. And while you may be tempted to take less than 12 months, don't do it. Even though you are helping people out of a financial jam and by extension strengthening the family and the community, you are not running a charity. This is a business. Twelve months. Nothing less. Preferably even more.

7. You will sell the home back to the clients in 3 years

If we assume that you have followed the steps in the strategy and that the tenants have been good and on time with their monthly payments, then you will be selling the home back to them in three years. The length of the agreement here is important. While I have done some refinances with longer terms, three years is the most efficient length of time. So the assumption here is that when you set up your refinance deal with your homeowners, you will be working with a three year term.

8. You want an annualized return of at least 20%

Because investing in any kind of real estate opportunity carries some risk—not even the 7-Step Lease Option Refinance Strategy can eliminate all risk—it's important that the potential reward be significant. In this strategy, we expect double digit returns and, moreover, we expect to gain at least 20% per year on average, over the course of the term.

9. You will reinvest your proceeds again

This assumption is completely optional and will definitely depend on your own personal circumstances, but if you are young or in your middle-ages and are looking at this strategy as a way to build wealth for future retirement or a life of leisure, then you'll want to take the proceeds of your first deal and reinvest them into another 7-Step Lease Option Refinance Strategy deal. By reinvesting the profits now, you will build wealth faster than most, and safer than most, and with a lot less work than most.

10. How you make money

In the 7-Step Lease Option Refinance Strategy, you will make money three ways. First, you will collect a commission for your services up front when you purchase the investment property. You can choose whatever commission you like, but I have found that 5% is completely acceptable. Homeowners understand that this is typically what they would pay to a real estate agent anyway if they sold their home.

Next, you will be collecting a return on your investment every month. Your tenants will be paying you a return, typically double digit. What this means is that you don't have to wait for the end of the term in order to realize a return on your investment. You make money every time you cash a rent cheque.

Finally, you will make money at the end of the lease option refinance term when you sell the property back to the tenant.

Three ways to make money:
- 5% commission paid up front on closing
- monthly returns every time you cash a rent cheque
- more cash at the end of the term when you sell the property

What other investments can boast that kind of ongoing monetization?

Chapter Highlights

- As the investor, you make money up front, during the lease term, and at the end of the term. These returns are normally

at least 20% per year.
- Your risks are minimized with lease option agreements and with 12 months of expenses held by you in reserve. These funds come from the tenant's equity when you purchase the property from him. By following the 7-Step Lease Option Refinance Strategy, your overall investment risks will be minimized.

The 7-Step Lease Option Refinance Strategy

Chapter 3

What is a Real Estate Lease Option, and How Does it Work?

Argue for your limitations and sure enough, they're yours.

Richard Bach

At the heart of the 7-Step Lease Option Refinance Strategy is a lease option agreement between you the investor, and the homeowner who needs a solution. When you agree to purchase a property from a homeowner, thereby making them your tenants, you put in place an agreement that provides them with the option of purchasing the home back at the end of the term. It's the kind of agreement that is used in numerous real estate transactions and for other leased assets like vehicles or furniture.

But there is always a bit of confusion around what a lease option agreement really is, so I want to outline the basic principles of the lease option, so that you are well-versed when discussing it with mortgage brokers and homeowners.

The lease option agreement is a binding contract between the tenant and the landlord (that would be you as owner of the property). In order to have a valid option the client provides "valuable consideration" (that is, a fee) for the option to purchase their home back. In other words, the tenant is going to provide a large amount of money from his equity in order to maintain the first right of refusal when you sell the property in three years. That protects the tenant from you just selling it to anyone at any time. And, it protects you so that you know that you already have a buyer for the property, and if the tenant does not fulfill his end of the agreement, he will forfeit his option to you.

In the 7-Step Lease Option Refinance Strategy, this consideration that the tenant provides is called the Purchase Option, which, if the tenant exercises it, is used as a down payment in the repurchase of the home.

The key elements of a lease option agreement are as follows.

The Buyer purchases the option

The parties (that's you and the tenant) agree to what the cost, or amount, of the purchase option is. In the 7-Step Lease Option Refinance Strategy, we are going to insist on having at least 12 months of expenses covered, so the amount of the purchase option will be just that: 12 months of expenses. So when you're crunching numbers on a deal to see if it will work or not, you will add up all your expenses for a year and this will be the purchase option amount.

But this is not "free money" for you. And I should tell you to be wary of real estate investment companies or brokers that try to tell you that a tenant's purchase option is money in your pocket. It isn't. The purchase option will go back to the tenant at the end of the refinance term if and only if he meets all his obligations under your agreement with him. While he is in your agreement, the money from the purchase option is held by you, and it may be tempting to look at this as "free money". But in your agreement with the tenant, you will specify that the only time it can be accessed is if you need it to cover a missed rent payment, or if the tenant needs to be evicted, or for any other reason leading to the tenant breaking his agreement with you. In other words, the funds are to be held for the tenant unless the tenant is in breach of his agreement.

Now this next part is extremely important, so I'm going to use squiggly writing to emphasize it: *The purchase option fee is non-refundable. That is, if the client fails to exercise the option to buy back the home at the end of the term, the money goes to you. It is not refunded to the tenant. The reason is that the purchase option fee is not a deposit. The option fee has been used to purchase something of value: the option.*

This is another reason why we want to have at least 12 months of expenses covered in the purchase option: it is a strong incentive for the tenant to stick with the agreement and to purchase the property back in three years.

Listen. You are not in the long-term rental property business. You do not want to hold onto these properties forever. So you are looking for ways to make sure the tenant sticks with the agreement and doesn't leave you with an empty house. The incentive is cold hard cash and lots of it. If the tenant knows that he will forfeit this cash if he doesn't exercise the option to purchase—for whatever reason—he will lose that money.

Agreed-to Repurchase Price

As part of the agreement between you and the tenant, you will agree on what the repurchase price will be at the end of the three year term. This is sometimes difficult to estimate because there are no crystal balls and no one can predict what the future will hold. But there are things we can do to come up with a realistic and practical repurchase price that is acceptable to all parties.

Some companies that offer lease option refinancing will purposely use a high repurchase price that, frankly, the tenant has no way of paying. Unethical operators do this with the hope that the tenant will have to walk away and not exercise the option at the end of the term so they can not only keep the purchase option funds, but also have an asset they can sell and gain from. There are some nasty operators around and if you stay in this business for any length of time, you will meet up with them. The thing about this strategy is that if you're honest and open and transparent in your dealings, you will develop a lot of trust and people every where will recognize that and will want to work with you. Only you.

Anyway, back to figuring out the repurchase price. There's an art to it. You want to maximize your profits of course, but you also need to ensure that the tenant can actually afford to buy the home back. In my experience, I've found that if you keep the repurchase price reasonable, you will not only improve the chances of the tenant completing the program, but you will also make some good profits.

To estimate the repurchase price, assuming the property is in a good economic area, I start with the rate of inflation and go from there. If inflation is running at 2% and the area is generally stable, I may go up to an annual appreciation rate of 2.5% or even 3%. If the property is in a high growth area, I'll go higher, say up to 4% annual market appreciation. Mortgage brokers and other real estate professionals can help you with this too.

The bottom line here is that both you and the tenant will agree to this repurchase price. Remember that the tenant will be a bit stressed here—he's gone through a lot with trying to save his home—and it would be unethical to take advantage of that. But if you're fair and you can show the tenant how you arrived at a reasonable repurchase price, then he will at least understand you're not trying to take advantage.

Once you have agreed on the repurchase price, this figure will go into the Purchase Option Agreement that you sign with the tenant up front so that everything is clear.

The length of the term: three years

As discussed in the previous chapter, the refinance term, or option period, is three years. This time is used to help the client get back on his financial feet through credit repair and for him to qualify for a new mortgage in order to repurchase the property. While some tenants feel they can do this in 6 months, my experience is that three years is a more realistic time frame.

Monthly Occupancy Fee

A lease option agreement requires a monthly lease payment that is often referred to as the "monthly occupancy fee". It is the fee paid by the tenant for the privilege of occupying the property—the same as rent—and is determined from the actual monthly expenses comprising mortgage payments, property tax, insurance, your monthly return, and property management.

The above five expense elements are real cost values. Nothing is made up here, so the tenant again understands exactly what he is paying for and why. If the tenant doesn't want to pay that much, you simply walk away. There are so many potential tenants out there that if anyone balks at the amount of the purchase option or the monthly occupancy fee, then you simply move on to the next one. Remember, you're not running a charity. All you need to do is stick with your operating assumptions and follow the steps in the 7-Step Lease Option Refinance Strategy. Don't ever feel that you need to adjust your investment parameters for anyone. You don't.

There are plenty of other clauses in the lease option agreement that address such items as ongoing maintenance, who will occupy the property, late fees for NSF cheques, and so on. We will go through these clauses in Chapter 4: Step 4.

The lease option agreement is a very powerful tool but it is not to be entered into lightly. You will need to understand everything in your agreements. And, you will need to make sure that your lawyer reviews it so that nothing is left out. When I prepare a lease option agreement with an option to purchase for my tenants, everything is accounted for and is clearly presented to them. You'll be doing the same thing with this strategy too. And just to make sure the tenant doesn't feel he's ever being taken advantage of, I ask all tenants to seek independent legal advice before they sign the agreement in order to assure themselves of its contents and their obligations and privileges.

Chapter Highlights

- In a lease option, the client—in this case, the tenant—pays you a fee in consideration of having the first right of refusal when you sell the property. In this way, when he exercises the option, his fee is credited towards the purchase of the property. If he doesn't exercise the option, he loses his fee.
- Lease option agreements are fairly complex, but in

general they comprise what the repurchase price of the property will be, how much the option fee is, and how long the lease term will be.
- During the lease option term, the homeowner-tenant stays in the home. He does not have to move, and, with his option fee, he will have the first right of refusal to purchase the property back.

Chapter 4

The 7-Step Lease Option Refinance Strategy

A creative man is motivated by the desire to achieve, not by the desire to beat others.

Ayn Rand

Refinancing Existing Homeowners

In the 7-Step Lease Option Refinance Strategy, we are only going to work with existing homeowners who are generally established in their communities and have built up some equity in their homes.

As you know, the lease option strategy is used in a variety applications, from leasing cars to furniture. It is also used in "rent to own" or "lease to own" real estate scenarios. These situations arise typically when someone wants to buy a property—usually a young couple—and they either don't have a sufficient down payment, or else their credit is bad and they can't secure a mortgage.

The 7-Step Lease Option Refinance Strategy

I've done a couple of rent to own purchase deals with new home buyers and although I might consider doing some again, they are much riskier than dealing with existing home owners. Why is that? Quite simply, the existing homeowner has more to lose if he doesn't fulfill his obligations than someone who puts little money down. Moreover, the 7-Step Lease Option Refinance Strategy counts on having at least 12 months of expenses held in reserve. These funds come from the homeowner's equity. A rent to own person simply doesn't have that kind of cash and, therefore, is a higher risk.

Remember, we not only want to make money from day 1; we also want to make sure we don't lose money. Ever! The best way to ensure that we don't is to have a large reserve fund, solid agreements, and great investment deals.

There are other advantages to working with existing homeowners. Chances are they have families and are well-entrenched in their communities. That is, they may be involved in coaching kids' sports or helping out at the local school. They have a stake in staying in their home and are willing to do whatever it takes in order to stay there. Let's face it: no one wants to have to pull their kids out of school, up-root the family and move to a rental. The 7-Step Lease Option Refinance Strategy offers a way for them to keep their homes while getting back on their financial feet.

The following subchapters outline the strategy in specific detail.

Step 1

Identify Your Investment Funds

In this first step, we're going to take a closer look at where you can find the investment funds you need in order to fully maximize your profits under the 7-Step Lease Option Refinance Strategy. As I've mentioned previously, my assumption is that you have about $100k that you can invest. So, clearly, this is not a no money down strategy. It is a real life strategy and is best suited to those who have equity built up in their homes and/or other investment funds available.

For the purpose of demonstration, I will assume that you are a homeowner, and that you have built up some equity in your home. You are employed and hopefully you enjoy your work, because this strategy is not about quitting your job in six months so you can lie on a beach somewhere (we'll leave those ideas for late night television).

Let us also assume that you have some savings put away. Maybe you have a pension plan at work or you've taken advantage of a government savings plan. Be assured, we aren't going to be looking at those savings. You want to keep those safe for when you do retire.

The way we're going to maximize the 7-Step Lease Option

Refinance Strategy is through the use of a home equity line of credit.

The Home Equity Line of Credit (HELOC)

If you own your home and are gainfully employed, it's quite likely that you'll be able to get yourself a home equity line of credit, or HELOC for short. This is the easiest and cheapest money to find, other than if you kept cash in your bank account. Why is this? For starters, the amount of the HELOC is based on the appraised value of your home and how much outstanding debt you have on it. So for example, if your home is appraised at $400,000 and you owe $200,000 on your outstanding mortgage, the equity in your home is the difference… $200,000. You won't get a HELOC at that value, because your bank or other lender will not give you that much. But typically, a bank will lend you up to 80% of the value of your home.

So in this example, if your lender is willing to lend up to 80% LTV (loan to value, i.e., the ratio of debt to the value of your home), we will get:

$400,000 X 0.8 = $320,000

MINUS $200,000 outstanding mortgage

EQUALS $120,000 available for your HELOC

What this means is that, once the HELOC is in place, you can draw down on it just like you would a credit card, and you only get charged interest when there is an outstanding debt.

However, you will undoubtedly see the potential problem with this much of a line of credit. There is always the temptation to treat this as "free money". It is not. You will only be using this HELOC for investment purposes and nothing else, and you will need to be disciplined with this or else you could end up in a serious financial dilemma.

To calculate how much of a HELOC you could obtain, the easiest thing is to go to the following website:

http://www.calcxml.com/calculators/how-much-can-i-borrow-from-my-home-equity-heloc

and put your own numbers into it. Aside: Just a quick note on website addresses used here… as you know, websites are constantly changing, so be sure to check my personal website at www.HootInvest.com for the latest updates. Getting back to our example, unless you have undertaken an appraisal of your home recently, you may not really know its value. Try not to over-estimate its worth. It's always best to be conservative in all these calculations.

You will also have to speak with your bank or financial institution to see how much of a HELOC they are willing to provide you, that is, what is the maximum loan to value (LTV). Many institutions will give you up to 80%. Some may go as high as 90%. You may wish to shop around to find the best rate at the highest LTV.

Once you have this information, it will be easy to calculate the amount of HELOC you should be able to obtain.

There are costs to put a HELOC in place. Typically, you will need to pay for the appraisal and for the legal work to register the HELOC against your property. This could cost upwards of $500, but the cost is well worth it considering what you're going to be able to do with the line of credit.

For the sake of this demonstration, let us suppose that you are able to secure a $120,000 HELOC. But, because we want to preserve cash as much as we want to make cash, we will never use up all of this line of credit. We will always hold some of it open in case there is an emergency of some sort. So let's suppose we will only commit up to $100,000 for investment purposes, and the rest will be left alone.

Calculating how much property you can purchase

Now that you know how much you have to invest, you can calculate the maximum amount of property you can purchase. Use the following formula to calculate this:

Your available investment funds DIVIDED BY (the amount of down payment + closing costs, in percentages)

As an example, assume that you are going to get a 75% loan to value new first mortgage on your investment property. This means you will have to put a down payment of 25% on the property. Now estimate your closing costs to be 3% (closing costs are all those other expenses that you will need to pay in order to close your purchase. These comprise things like legal fees, disbursements, title searches, title insurance, and so on. A good estimate for these fees is 3% of the purchase price, but that can vary depending on where the property is located, so it's always best to check with an experienced mortgage broker or real estate agent).

Using the above formula, we find:

Maximum property value = $100,000 / (0.25 + 0.03)

= $100,000 / 0.28

= $357,142

For the purpose of this demonstration, let's round that off to $350,000 because, again, it's always best to be conservative when it comes to investing. In other words, if you have a HELOC of $120,000 on your home, you can afford an investment property of $350,000.

Other sources of funds

If you do not have sufficient equity in your home to obtain $100k of investment funds, then you need to look at other sources. Here are a few ideas that you could consider, but remember, one of the benefits of using borrowed cash for investment purposes is that you will likely realize some excellent tax advantages. Be sure to discuss your plans with an experienced tax accountant.

Other cash savings

If you have cash savings in your bank, then you can certainly use these for investment purposes. That said, you always want to make sure you have an emergency fund available in case something goes horribly wrong because, let's face it, life happens.

Liquidating assets

Do you have things around the house that you can sell? Perhaps you have other investments that aren't performing very well… could you liquidate some of them into cash?

You may want to make a list of all your assets and determine which ones you could liquidate to free up some extra cash. A list of assets is always a good thing to have and you'll need one in order to calculate your net worth when you go to qualify for a mortgage anyway.

Have a look at investments, furniture, cars, cottages, boats, jewelry, or anything else that you could sell for cash. When you begin to add these up, you may find that you do indeed have plenty of cash available.

Pooling funds with other family members

Suppose you have $40,000 and your siblings or parents would be willing to go in with you on a lease option refinance property. You can pool your funds and divide up the profits according to how much each person contributes.

If you do this, it is imperative that you have a lawyer draw up an agreement so that you, your family and the income-generating asset are protected. As well, the bank that's going to provide you with a first mortgage will want to see the financial status of your "partners" too, since they will also have to qualify.

This is not an easy way to do things. Any investment involving family members could easily turn sour and make for awkward suppers together at Thanksgiving. I know some investors who simply refuse to go in with family members for this very reason.

A word on credit cards

There are some real estate investment teachers who will push you into using credit card cash advances to buy property. The idea here is that you may be able to qualify for an increase in your credit limit, and if your credit history is good, you may be able to secure $100,000 in credit cards reasonably quickly and easily.

But beware! The interest charged on credit cards is outrageous compared to what you'll get charged on a HELOC or even what you might get charged from a private lender. They may seem easy and quick and painless, but using credit cards for investments is a very dangerous proposition. I recommend you stay away from them altogether, and if someone tells you there's no harm in using them for investments, just walk away.

Private money

Since we don't want to use credit cards at all for investment purposes, there is another place to go for money and that's a private money source. Now, I'm not talking about the local loan shark here who might send "Butch" to visit you if you're late on a payment… no. I'm talking about bona fide private lenders. You can sometimes find their advertisements in the local classifieds, and your mortgage broker, accountant or lawyer might know a few that they can recommend too.

The advantage to working with a private lender is they usually are not as onerous to deal with as banks. Sure, they will want to see some collateral and they'll need to see your financial history and your assets just like any lender, but they can usually provide you as much as you need—if not more—without having to go through all the hoops that the bank will set up for you.

The drawback to working with private lenders is they charge a higher interest rate than a bank. As well, they don't normally like to lend their cash out for more than 12 months at a time, so a three year commitment (which is the length of time for the lease option refinance term) may not be attractive to them.

Still, they are a viable option and I know investors who have used private lenders for some or all of their investment funds.

But having said all that, the best way to secure investment funds is through a HELOC, which is why we make getting one a significant part of the 7-Step Lease Option Refinance Strategy.

Step 1 Highlights

- The home equity line of credit (HELOC) is your best vehicle for obtaining investment money, other than cash in a bank account.

Step 1 – Identify Your Investment Funds

- With $100,000 you will be able to purchase an investment property of $350,000.
- Be sure to discuss tax strategies with your accountant in order to set up your business effectively.

Step 2

Select Your Team of Experts

Too often when you read books about investing in real estate, the focus is on you. Sure, you need to do a lot of work—no question about it—but what's missing is the fact that you don't have to do it alone. Moreover, you shouldn't do this alone! Unless, of course, you just happen to be an expert in the 7-Step Lease Option Refinance Strategy (which you will be), *and* an expert in mortgages, real estate law and contracts, accounting and bookkeeping, client relations, property management, home insurance, administration… you get the picture.

Under the 7-Step Lease Option Refinance Strategy, you will be the lease option refinance expert. You will have all the information you need to answer just about any question that comes up (and if you can't find the answer, then contact me at david@cardinalhomeinvestments.com and I will find the answer for you. See, for real, you are not alone in this!). Since you will be the lease option refinance expert, you will need to work with other real estate professionals to provide you with professional advice and expertise. This is how it should be, since no one can really expect to know everything about everything there is to know about making money in real estate.

Let's recall what it is we're trying to accomplish here. We want to make above average returns on a secured investment without taking on a lot of risk. Moreover, we don't want to be managing this investment full-time and we certainly don't want to be called up every time the tenant has a problem.

To accomplish this goal, we're going to rely on a team of professionals that you get to pick, and this comprises Step 2 of the strategy. Here is a breakdown of those experts that you'll want on your side.

Mortgage broker professional

A key member of your team is the mortgage broker professional. This person will work closely with you to identify qualified homeowners for the 7-Step Lease Option Refinance Strategy, and they will also help you find the best mortgage available for your property.

A mortgage broker can do more for you than just submit your mortgage application to a bunch of lenders and wait for their responses. A good broker will also provide you with expertise and guidance on how best to prepare your mortgage application for different lenders, what terms and conditions to be wary of, and how to make sure you get exactly what you need in your mortgage.

As well, the mortgage broker is the one who can find qualified homeowners who can benefit from the service you are offering. Let's think about why this is. First, if you are a homeowner and your bank won't renew your mortgage, what would you do? Most people would go to their nearest mortgage broker to see if they can find another lender to help them out. So, as professionals on the front lines of mortgages and refinancing, brokers are usually some of the first to hear about potential tenants for you. If you tell them exactly what you're looking for and how the 7-Step Lease Option Refinance Strategy works (remember, you will be the expert in this), then the broker can filter out deals on your behalf and send potential tenants your way for qualification.

Will this cost you anything? The mortgage broker gets paid whenever she puts a new mortgage in place. So if you give her your business and ask her to find a mortgage for your new income property, she will be thrilled with that. However, if you are also asking her to go fishing for potential opportunities, filter out clients and assist in some of the qualifying process, then it makes sense to pay her something extra. I like to pay the brokers I work with $500 for a referral fee. That is, if a broker sends me a potential tenant and that tenant qualifies and enters into a lease option arrangement with me, then I'll pay the broker a $500 referral fee and I will also try to put my mortgage through them too.

Selecting a mortgage broker

There are two types of brokers that you will likely work with at some point. The first might be your local broker… one who lives in your community that you can go and visit and discuss real estate investing with. The other may be in a totally different community, that is, in a community that you have targeted for investment.

Let's suppose you live in London, Ontario but your research tells you that you really want to invest in the growing community of Calgary, Alberta. You'll be able to do a lot of good things with your local broker, but chances are you will end up working with a broker in Calgary because they are closer to the market in Calgary, obviously, and therefore more aware of who might benefit from your service.

This is not always the case, especially these days with internet access and 24/7 availability. But if you really want to invest in Calgary, it just makes sense to identify some key brokers in that community to work with.

While the mortgage broker community is becoming more and more professional, there are still all kinds of brokers out there so you have to do some homework to find a few that you can work with. The best broker for finding potential tenants is the broker who does the most business. That's a pretty simple strategy: find the brokers who do the most business. Then, look for the reviews by satisfied clients to see how they liked the experience. Most of these will be from clients who are looking to qualify themselves—not investors—so you will need to talk to a few people to see how different brokers operate.

Some things you want to look for in a broker are the following:
- Are they accredited brokers? That is, do they belong to a professional organization with ethical and professional standards?
- Do they have a team of junior brokers working with them that they'll push you on, or will you be working directly with the primary broker?
- Do they understand the 7-Step Lease Option Refinance Strategy and what you are looking for? If you're not sure, ask them to pretend that you are a homeowner looking for a solution to your mortgage problem, and have them explain the lease option strategy to you.
- Are they investors themselves or do they work with other investors? This might be helpful in determining whether the broker understands what your goals are.

Finally, one of the most important things in determining who to work with is whether you feel there is a good personality fit between you and the broker. You need to be able to trust that the broker will be open and honest with you at all times, and you need to feel assured that you are getting the best advice and expertise possible. This also goes for all the others on your team.

Bookkeeper

If you haven't guessed by now, your application of the 7-Step Lease Option Refinance Strategy is akin to running a part-time business. It's really important to keep all of your personal expenses separate from your real estate expenses and revenues. If you do that up front before you purchase your investment property, you'll save yourself a ton of headaches at tax time.

A good bookkeeper will help you set up your accounts properly and will provide you with some assistance in tracking your expenses so you can keep a sharp eye on the performance of your investment. Between the bookkeeper and the accountant, you may be able to identify certain household expenses that you can claim a portion of as a reasonable business expense, for example, if you have a home office.

So unless you're already an experienced business person, accountant or bookkeeper, you will need to find a solid bookkeeper—preferably one who has some experience with real estate investors or home-based businesses. Your local classifieds or kijiji should give you some leads, or perhaps your mortgage broker or accountant can help you with a couple of recommendations.

Accountant

While the bookkeeper will track day to day operational expenses, the accountant is the one who will prepare your tax returns and provide you with advice related to advantageous tax strategies. Accountants cost money, of course, so you don't want the accountant to do anything that the bookkeeper can do. But you do want to make sure the accountant understands real estate investment and especially the 7-Step Lease Option Refinance Strategy.

Just as an example, when you collect the purchase option cash from your tenant—worth tens of thousands of dollars—is it considered taxable income? The answer should be no, because it is not income: it is being held on behalf of the tenant and will be returned once he completes his agreement. Your accountant will be able to structure this kind of transaction to ensure that you don't pay any more tax than you are legally obliged to pay.

Again, just like you do with the bookkeeper, it is best to meet with your accountant before you purchase your property to make sure that your investment business is set up properly from the start. This will potentially save you a lot of money and frustration later on.

Real estate lawyer

Next on your team is a real estate lawyer. There are lots of good lawyers around so you shouldn't have any trouble finding an individual or a firm that can help you out. The key selection criteria for you with a lawyer is to make sure you are dealing with someone who specializes in real estate. There are plenty of general law practitioners around, but you want someone who is familiar not only with the transactional requirement of buying and selling properties, but also familiar with lease option law, provincial or state eviction laws, and any other related regulations in your jurisdiction. You will also want someone who can review your agreements and ensure they are applicable in the jurisdiction where you're buying your income property. While the general lease option laws are similar across the country, there are local variations and only an experienced lawyer will know what to look for and to make your agreements bullet-proof.

Property manager

At some point soon, you will need to decide whether you want to manage your income property yourself, or have a professional property manager do it on your behalf. If you're a hands-on type who doesn't mind dealing with tenants and taking monthly trips to your property to make sure it's being looked after, then you might want to do it all yourself. This will save you some money too. On the other hand, you may have no desire at all to be involved in chasing tenants who pay late, or eviction processes, or anything else like that. In this case, you'll want a professional property manager to work on your behalf.

Good property management firms will offer you a variety of services for a variety of different fees. It's important to know what you will be looking for up front when you speak with a property manager, so they can help identify the right services for you.

When you have a tenant in place and your refinance term is underway, you should not need a lot of hands-on work if everything is running smoothly. All you will need is for someone to drive by the property once a month, take some pictures of the property, and check in with the tenants. This will give you assurances that the property is being looked after by the tenant and that there aren't all of a sudden 20 people living there.

But this assumes that everything is running smoothly. Life happens, and sometimes your tenants will be late with their rent or they will ask you to hold off cashing the rent cheque for a couple of weeks. In my experience, some tenants will start asking you right away for a "break" or a favour, and they will come up with a hundred different excuses for not paying you on time. When this happens, managing the tenants yourself is a real source of stress.

So this is how it will work if you decide to go with a property manager. You will collect all the rent cheques up front when you buy the investment property, and you will cash them monthly yourself in your own bank account. You will hire a property manager to do the following:

- Drive by the property once a month, take a few pictures of the property and, if they have a chance, meet with the tenant for a 5 minute walk-through of the property. The property manager will then send you these pictures and a very brief report—by email—so you have a record of good management on the property. Plus, if the property manager detects something that looks out of place or inconsistent, he can alert you to that for your own follow up.

- Along with this monthly requirement, you also want the property manager to initiate eviction proceedings immediately if a rent cheque is NSF or if the tenant is otherwise in breech of his agreement with you. The property manager will tell you what it will cost to begin an eviction process and he will detail for you everything that he will do to evict your tenants. This may sound drastic: starting an eviction process if a rent cheque happens to bounce, but let me assure you, you will rue the day you let one cheque slip by a few days or weeks. To tenants, this will be a weak link that they will consistently exploit. They need to know that you are running a serious business, and that your lease option refinance service is serious too. Any slip up, and eviction proceedings will begin.

The property manager may have other services to offer you as well, and you can certainly discuss these with him, but the above two are the most important: have someone do the monthly monitoring on the property, and someone who will start eviction proceedings immediately. No ifs ands or buts!

Contractors

Last but not least on your team is a good all around handyman who can do some light contract work such as painting, fixing a door, replacing a window or things like that. The tenant is responsible for all maintenance of the property during the lease option refinance term, but you never know when you might need someone to help out with something, especially if the tenants move out and you need to fix a few things in the property before selling it.

You may already know one or two contractors who do good work on your own home. Next time you see them, mention to them that you will be investing in real estate and that you might need their services later. They will be glad to do some extra work for you.

In choosing a contractor, you need someone who is honest and trustworthy and who will be available relatively quickly and whose rates are competitive. In the case of contractors, recommendations from friends are really important. When choosing contractors, I'm more interested in those I can trust to get the job done quickly and well, than I am about price. Remember, if the tenants do move out, they forfeit their purchase option and you will have access to that to get the property spruced up and ready for the market.

Trusted Advisor

The next member of your team is a trusted advisor. This person does not have to be a real estate investor—although that can help—they simply need to be an experienced you person you trust for sound, objective advice.

The other professionals on your team will be happy to help you, naturally, and they will give you advice related to their specific areas of expertise, but you also need someone available to talk to about other things…things like business strategy, planning, working with others, or just bouncing ideas off of. This is where your trusted advisor comes in.

I know many investors who have no idea who to turn to for this kind of advice. Often, family members are too close or pessimistic to be of much help. Business associates have their own worries and may not be all that interested in what you're doing. So where do you go next if you're looking for an advisor but don't really have anyone in mind?

One place you could look is your local real estate investment club or organization. Seek out the people who seem to be in constant demand and ask them if they know anyone. Another place could be your social network. Perhaps there are people in your community group that would be willing to meet with you from time to time to discuss investment business. Also, since this is what Cardinal Home Investments does, we have advisory services with many investors who are looking for some information or consultation. So, finding a trusted advisor should not be overly challenging.

The kind of relationship you want with an advisor really depends on what kind of personality you have and how much time your advisor has to spare. When I was starting out, my advisor and I met every couple of months for lunch to discuss our affairs and any issues I was facing. That worked out well for me. Others require more frequent email contact or telephone calls. Remember, if this relationship is going to work well, it has to work for both of you, so take the time up front to define what the relationship will look like, and adjust as you go.

When you have contacted your team members, you will be able to move forward with your investment program in confidence. So right now would be a good time to make a record of your team members along with their coordinates. You can then copy this page and tack it up at your desk so that it's always close by.

List of Team Members

Name	Expertise	Address	Telephone	Email
	Broker			
	Bookkeeper			
	Accountant			
	Lawyer			
	Property Manager			
	Contractor			
	Advisor			
	Other			
	Other			

Step 2 Highlights

- You are not expected to do all this by yourself. Having a team of experts by your side plays an important role in your ongoing investment success.
- Establish an ongoing relationship with a trusted advisor— someone you can talk to about your business and any significant issues that may come your way.

Step 3

Find a Qualified Property

Now that you have secured your investment funds of $100k and identified your team of experts, the third step in the 7-Step Lease Option Refinance Strategy is to find a suitable property for refinance. In this chapter, we're going to look at the key selection criteria that you should follow in order to minimize your risks and maximize your success. Then, we'll look at some ways that you can market your service to mortgage brokers and potential homeowners. Shall we begin?

In my experience with real estate investing, there are three areas that have the most risk for you: bad tenants, a bad property, and not enough funds held in reserve. What happened to me when I first began investing was typical, I think. I was so anxious to put a couple of deals together and get in the real estate game that I made several poor investment decisions. I bought ugly properties with horrible tenants and never had enough cash in reserve to carry more than a couple of months of expenses. It was a nightmare, let me tell you. And a costly one too.

With those dark days well behind me now, I have done the only thing I could do, and that is learn as much as I could from those mistakes and build a strategy that directly addresses those three dangerous areas. I then incorporated those ideas into the 7-Step Lease Option Refinance Strategy.

Qualifying property criteria

When we talk about finding a suitable property, we mean finding a property that meets certain selection criteria. The same is true for the homeowners, and we'll look at their criteria in the next section. For now, though, let's focus on selecting a good property.

All of these criteria work to your benefit. If you follow them exactly, you will reduce the risk in the 7-Step Lease Option Refinance Strategy. They have been developed over the past several years and fire-tested in the real world. Over time, the ones that didn't work were turfed out and replaced with others that did work. What we have now may change in the future too, depending on economic conditions or other realities, but for now, these have been working very well.

The criteria have also been divided up into "mandatory" and "evaluated", with the idea being that if a property does not meet all of the mandatory criteria, it is rejected right then and there. If the property meets the mandatory criteria, then the others are evaluated. In this way, the property that scores the highest should give you the best risk mitigation.

Let's have a look at the mandatory criteria first. Remember, at this point we aren't even considering the tenants yet, just the property. The tenants come later!

Mandatory Property Criteria	Yes or No
Single family home	
Not a condominium	
Not a mobile home or trailer	
Municipal water and sewer	
In an economically stable or growing community	
No major repairs required	
Price is in the middle	

Single family home

We've talked about this earlier in the book. The only types of property that we are interested in are single family homes, so this criteria is first on the list of mandatories. If the property is not a single family home, move on. 'Nuff said.

Not a condominium

This is another really important mandatory requirement, and I know what some of you are thinking. You're thinking, what could possibly be so wrong about a condominium, especially some of the newer ones? I know we've been over this ground briefly in our list of assumptions back in Chapter 2, but let's go over this again and differentiate between some of these condos. An apartment condominium is simply not on our list. These are not single family homes. They are apartments. Despite what the media reports and other real estate investors may tell you, stay away from apartment condos. They simply don't work well for the 7-Step Lease Option Refinance Strategy because there are too many variables that are outside of our control and that fact alone renders the risk too high.

Next, let's look at some condos that you might think could work. There are several older developments of row houses or town houses that are condos. You've seen them around, I'm sure. While these are single family homes, the problem is they are still condos!

I need to make this really clear: when you're dealing with a condo, you are giving up control of your asset to a board of directors who could care less about you or your 7-Step Lease Option Refinance Strategy. They will do what's in the best interest of the entire development—especially if they benefit. So you can expect all kinds of calls on your cash for emergencies and landscaping and new roofs and pools and play structures and so on. And you will not have any say in the matter if the board of directors approves these things.

Moreover, condominium associations are usually governed by provincial or state laws, and whenever government is involved in the running of things, bad stuff can happen. Is that a generalization? You bet. Is it true anyway? Absolutely.

You know, I have a friend who always used to tell me that if I go out looking for trouble, chances are I'll find it. Naturally, I had to prove this statement wrong so I went out looking for trouble and, alas, despite my best efforts, I either found trouble or it found me! Lesson learned.

So let's not invite trouble. We will avoid condos completely.

Not a mobile home or trailer

Once people find out about your service, you will start getting queries from all kinds of folks all over the place. Sooner or later you will be asked whether your lease option refinance service applies to mobile homes or trailers. The answer is no. 'Nuff said again.

Okay well if you really want to know, mobile homes are deadly difficult to sell if your tenants take off. The land they sit on is normally not owned: it is leased. This means you don't own it and the problems associated with condo corporations also apply here too. Besides, really, if you want to earn money on a solid investment that you can take some pride in, why would you ever invest in a mobile home?

Municipal water and sewer

This criteria is a mandatory one for the simple reason that the alternative—septic tanks and wells—are not always reliable and require constant upkeep and servicing. So it's easier to stick with properties that are on municipal water and sewers.

This is not to say that there aren't some really nice properties on septic tanks and well water… there are! But remember, this is about minimizing your risks as an investor. And even though the tenant is responsible for the upkeep and maintenance of the property during the refinance term, if a septic tank needs to be replaced, you can be sure that you will be asked to help pay for it. And if there are any health issues associated with it, the municipality will come after you since you the owner.

Again, let's avoid potential problems whenever we can. Stick with municipal water and sewers.

Step 3 – Find a Qualified Property

In an economically stable or growing community

Of all the mandatory criteria, this is perhaps the one that most investors have difficulty with.

First, in order to determine whether a community is economically stable, you need to do some homework. You will need to look for those factors that contribute to a strong community:

- Population growth
- Job creation and growth
- Diversified economy
- Low vacancy rates
- New highways or other infrastructure

To find this information, you may need to contact the local chamber of commerce in the community you're considering, and spend some time reading the financial reports for that region. But chances are, you already know what areas of the region or country are expanding and which ones are not.

So that's the first thing: you need to do some homework.

The second reason why this criteria is difficult is purely emotional, and when it comes to investing your money, emotion must avoided. You must care only about preserving your money, and making more money.

What inevitably happens is an investor will want to invest in his own community, *whether it's an economically stable community or not!* And this is the problem. Too often, we get tied to our own cities and towns emotionally because we live there. We tell ourselves that, even though times might not be great right now, they will be soon, and besides, there are some really nice neighbhourhoods around and surely someone could use my lease option refinance service.

That is why some investors from Detroit will still invest in Detroit properties even though the manufacturing sector has been in decline for years, and the city itself is in financial ruin. As an investor, you will need to eliminate the emotion from your investment decisions, and go where the economy is growing.

The reason for doing this is quite simple. If you have tenants that cannot complete their refinance terms, then you need to evict them and sell the property. In a growing community, you will have less trouble selling your home than if the community is in decline.

Growing community = more buyers = better prices. Declining community = fewer buyers = lower prices. This math is so simple, why, it's not even real math!

In the scenario where you have to sell your property early, you want to make sure you can sell it for a good price, and sell it quickly. So let's stick with investing in growing communities.

No major repairs required

The last of the mandatory criteria is a property that does not require any major repairs. When we're talking "major", we mean things like replacing a roof, or fixing the foundation or any of those big, structural items. Minor things like carpets and paint do not matter as much, but the last thing you want is to get someone into your lease option refinance term, only to find out that the furnace needs replacing, the shingles on the roof are curling, and the garage is starting to lean.

I'm often surprised at the number of investors who overlook these deficiencies—even though they are identified in a house inspection—because they want to be seen as good people helping out others in their time of need.

There is nothing wrong with charity or with helping others to get back on their feet. That's one of the things I really like about lease option refinancing. But our desire to help others must be tethered by our investment discipline. It is a far better service to be able to help someone complete the lease option refinance term and get back on their financial feet than it is to pity someone, put them into the strategy when you know there are problems with the property, and have them not succeed.

There are so many people who need help getting their finances together and who are falling behind in their mortgage payments. They are everywhere, too, and they come from all walks of life. There is no rush to jump on the first property you see. Make sure it fits the criteria so you can minimize your risk.

Price is in the middle

What do I mean by the price being in the middle? Simply, this means that you want to focus on properties that are neither too expensive nor too cheap. You want to find something in the middle of the price range in the area you're looking in, because that's where most of the home-buyers can be found.

Again, this is important in order to minimize your risk if you have to sell the property part way through the refinance term. If you buy a property that is too expensive, it may take you a long time to sell it because there simply aren't that many buyers looking for expensive homes. Conversely, if you buy something that's cheap, you may also find yourself having trouble attracting good buyers.

How do you determine what the middle price range is? You need to do some homework on your targeted community. Check on the internet to see what the average price is. Check what the average price is in specific neighbourhoods. Talk to a real estate agent or mortgage broker who is familiar with that area. Then you'll know whether you're in the middle or not.

In the example we've been using so far for the 7-Step Lease Option Refinance Strategy, we are looking at homes in the $350,000 range in major, growing urban centres. In the real world, for some communities, this will be too expensive and for others, it will be too cheap. So you will need to know your prices and your investment communities well.

And that's the list of mandatory criteria. You may wish to add to that list based on your own experience or risk tolerance, but for the vast majority of properties out there, if you follow these mandatory criteria, your risk will be significantly lowered. Again, at this point, we're only looking at the property—not the tenants.

Now let's consider some other criteria that are also important but where there is also some flexibility. These are what I call the "evaluated" criteria, because you can score them. Thus, if you have a few properties that all meet the mandatory criteria, these evaluated criteria will help you determine the least risky property among them.

Evaluated Property Criteria	Score
Overall desirability of the neighbourhood (1 = poor; 10 = fantastic)	
Fully detached home (10 points)	
Duplex (5 points)	
Freehold Town house (2 points)	
3 Bedrooms (10 points)	
< 3 bedrooms (3 points)	
4 bedrooms (5 points)	
> 4 bedrooms (2 points)	
Finished basement (10 points)	
No pool (10 points)	
New subdivision (10 points)	
Cul de sac (10 points)	
Crescent (7 points)	
Avenue or main street (3 points)	
Walking distance to public transit (10 points)	
TOTAL	

As with the mandatories, the evaluated criteria are based on how difficult it might be to sell the property if something goes wrong and you are forced to sell. You want to be able to get rid of the asset quickly, and there are some properties that sell faster than others.

Using the above criteria, the highest score a property could have is 70 points. Finding such a property might be challenging, but remember, the most important criteria are the mandatories. These evaluated criteria are simply designed to guide you when you're trying to decide between two or more potential ones.

So, a fully detached three-bedroom home, with a finished basement and no pool, on a cul de sac in a fantastic neighbourhood will be easier to sell than a 2 bedroom townhome on a busy street in a so-so neighbourhood. Makes sense, right?

You may wish to modify this list, of course, depending on your own experience and the investment region you're considering, as long as you maintaining an objective viewpoint. For example, it does not matter if *you* personally like swimming pools. What matters is knowing that homes with pools are harder to sell than homes without pools.

So, armed with your mandatory and evaluated property criteria, you should be able to quickly and easily qualify any given property in any given neighbourhood. But as you know, that's only part of the process. We also have to look closely at the homeowner-tenants.

Qualifying tenant criteria

Once we have qualified a property, we can focus on qualifying the tenant. In practice, I should mention, the qualification process goes back and forth between tenant and property. Sometimes your best qualified property does not have a qualified tenant, so there is some give and take when you're trying to find the opportunity that's right for you. But one thing is for sure: the either the property or the tenant does not meet the mandatory criteria, then there is no deal to be had.

As with the property criteria, there are both mandatory and evaluated criteria for the tenant as well. Let's start with the mandatories.

Mandatory Tenant Criteria	Yes or No
Tenant has sufficient equity in the property	
Tenant's total debt service ratio will be 43% maximum	
Tenant has stable income	
Tenant is not a chronic credit card abuser	
Tenant has a family in the home	

Tenant has sufficient equity in the property

It's clear that if the tenant does not have enough equity in his property to make the 7-Step Lease Option Refinance Strategy work, then there's no point in any further discussion no matter how nice the property is. You will run into people in this situation. They will live in a beautiful home but are so financial in trouble that there's no way this strategy will work for them.

Because their purchase option fee (which is also your security) comes from the equity in the home, you should be looking for families that have been in their homes for several years so that they have actually built up some equity over time.

You may be wondering how to figure out whether there is

sufficient equity or not. The way to do it is through the Lease Option Refinance Financial Analyzer, which is outlined in Chapter 5 and also available to my Platinum Members Investment Circle on www.HootInvest.com

Essentially, what you need to know for evaluating whether there is sufficient equity is the approximate value of the property, how much debt there is (including mortgages and consumer debts like car loans or credit cards), and what the approximate monthly occupancy fee will be. This is simple to evaluate with the Financial Analyzer. All you need from the tenant is:

- The approximate value of the property (an appraised value is best, but not always available); and
- How much debt is owed (mortgages plus consumer debts)

And that's it! From here, you can simply plug your numbers into the Financial Analyzer to determine whether the tenant has sufficient equity. If they don't and you start thinking about lowering the number of months of expenses you should have, don't do it. That's a signal to you that you're not being objective enough for your own good. There has to be at least 12 months of expenses covered in reserve / option payment to be accepted into the refinance strategy.

Tenant's total debt service ratio will be 43% maximum

The next mandatory to determine is the tenant's total debt service ratio (TDSR) *assuming* they are in the lease option refinance term. This will tell you whether or not they can actually afford your service, so the important thing to consider is not what their monthly payments are now, but what they will be assuming they are in the refinance term. The TDSR is generally calculated as follows:

$$TDSR = \frac{\text{annual mortgage payment} + \text{property tax} + \text{other debts}}{\text{gross family income}}$$

In the 7-Year Lease Option Refinance Strategy, when the tenant is in, he no longer has a mortgage payment and he does not pay the property tax (you do). What he does pay is his monthly occupancy fee, so we actually need to change the above formula to this:

$$\text{TDSR} = \frac{\text{annual occupancy fee} + \text{other annual debt payments}}{\text{gross family income}}$$

So in order to calculate this, we need to determine the annual occupancy fee, or at least get a good approximation. We do this through the Financial Analyzer to determine the monthly occupancy fee, and then multiply that by 12 months.

Why do we choose 43%? Again, this is a reflection of how much the tenant can afford to pay on a monthly basis. You could choose any other number, really. Banks, for example, tend to use 40% as the maximum TDSR. Private lenders may go up to 50%, but I think this is too risky for us. So, for this strategy, 43% is an appropriate maximum value for the TDSR.

Let's take a look at an example.

Suppose the tenant has a property valued at $300,000 and he has a mortgage on it for $175,000. He also has $20,000 in credit card debt that he needs to pay off, and $5,000 left on his car loan. But we assume that when he refinances, these other debts will be paid off.

Let's assume that his monthly occupancy fee under the lease option refinance is $2500, or $30,000 per year. We also assume that his total family income is $75,000 per year. With these numbers, we calculate the tenant's TDSR as follows:

$$\text{TDSR} = \frac{\$30,000 + \$0}{\$75,000}$$

$$= 40\%$$

At TDSR of 40% the tenant is well within our maximum value of 43%. So in this case, the tenant meets this mandatory criteria.

Tenant has stable income

The next mandatory criteria is that the tenant needs to have a stable income. This doesn't necessarily mean a salaried job, although that would be ideal. It simply means that the tenant needs to show gainful employment of some kind. Also, when we're looking at the "tenant", we mean that if there are two adults in the home, we would consider their combined incomes and both their jobs, as well as their combined debts.

As an example, suppose the husband is a contractor. He has steady work but some months are better than others. Let's also suppose his wife is a part-time supply teacher. Her hours also vary from month to month, but she can usually count on working 5 days per month during the school year.

Both of these incomes are okay because we're looking for stable income, that is, income that we can count on over the long-term even if it's not completely predictable on a monthly basis.

Tenant is not a chronic credit card abuser

One of the documents we look at closely in our evaluation of the tenant is the credit report. If you're working with a mortgage broker, he will probably already have a copy of this that he can share with you. The credit report contains a score which, frankly, is not that much of a concern to me because if their score was any good, then they wouldn't be having trouble finding a mortgage!

Personally, I'm not overly excited about credit scores. I know professionals and business owners with lousy credit, yet their incomes are healthy. That said, we do look at the tenant's credit report for one key reason, and that is to determine whether the tenant's financial problems are due to a singular event like a job loss or health problem, or whether they are caused by chronic abuse of credit cards and other borrowing.

If a tenant is in trouble because of a temporary setback like a job loss, we can help them. Their credit history will show that, other than this one blip, they are financially responsible and disciplined. On the other hand, there really isn't anything we can do for the chronic credit card abuser. This is the tenant who has a history of running up credit cards to their maximum limits, then missing monthly payments, and doing this over a long period of time.

Since our goal here is to minimize risk, it's best simply to avoid those tenants who cannot get their financial act together. Let's stick with those who have pride in meeting their financial obligations, and are only looking for a bit of help to get back on their feet.

Tenant has a family in the home

Finally, the last mandatory criteria is that the tenant has a family in the home, and preferably a family with kids that are in school. This is important for two reasons. First, it speaks to the tenant's motivation to keep his home. No one likes to uproot the family and move, especially if it involves changing schools for kids. Second, it is a lot harder for a family to up and leave in the middle of the night compared to a single guy or a childless couple. Again, this is all about minimizing your risks, and in my experience, families are less risky than singles or couples.

At one point, I had considered looking at the ages of the tenants as a mandatory criteria. This became a concern when my Cardinal colleagues and I were looking at an older couple who had run into financial trouble. She was in her late 50s and he was in his late 60s. Even though they would have benefitted financially from the 7-Step Lease Option Refinance Strategy, we felt that it was not in their best interest to take on a three year commitment and then get another 90% LTV mortgage at that stage in life. It made more sense for them to sell their home and down size into something more affordable.

This brings up the same point I've been making a few times in this book: just because you *can* put a lease option refinance deal together, doesn't mean you necessarily *should*. Some times, you just have to say "no" to people because the property isn't good enough, or because you really don't think it's in the tenant's best interest.

Now let's have a look at the evaluated criteria for the tenant. Here's the checklist I use:

Evaluated tenant criteria	Score
Tenant has lived in the community for at least 10 years (10 points)	
Tenant is involved in community volunteering (10 points)	
Tenant has one or more kids in grade school (10 points)	
Tenant has no or very little consumer debt (10 points)	
TOTAL	

There are fewer evaluated criteria for the tenant than there are for properties for the simple reason that there are more possible variations in properties. Still, the maximum score the tenant can have is 40 points, and if you are comparing several possible properties and tenants, this can help guide your decision.

When you complete your qualification screening of the property and the tenant, you will have two sets of mandatory criteria, and two sets of evaluated criteria. Obviously, both sets of mandatories must be met or else they simply do not qualify. But if you're looking at several properties that qualify on the mandatories, you should then combine the evaluated criteria scores to come up with a total for all. This will help guide your investment decision.

For example, suppose you are comparing three different properties and tenants. Let's assume that they all meet the mandatory requirements, so the only thing left to do is to look at which one carries the least amount of risk.

	Property 1	Property 2	Property 3
Property Scores	52	47	35
Tenant Scores	20	30	30
TOTAL	72	77	65

In the above scenario, even though all three properties/tenants qualify, the property with the least amount of risk to you is Property 2.

Now let's take a closer look at this and see what it really means. All three properties/tenants qualify for the 7-Step Lease Option Refinance Strategy. This means, no matter which one you choose to work with, they all minimize risk and offer you the best chance to make your profits without undue stress. Just because you chose the one that has the best chance of success, doesn't mean that the others aren't also good investments! So if you actually have more cash to invest than is required for Property 2, you may wish to think about investing in one of the others properties as well. In this way, you start to build your own real estate portfolio which, by definition, spreads the risk over several properties.

All of these criteria checklists are available free to my Platinum Members Investment Circle at www.HootInvest.com

Step 3 Highlights

- Use both mandatory and evaluated criteria to qualify both tenants and properties for the 7-Step Lease Option Refinance Strategy
- Where two or more potential opportunities are being evaluated, compare the evaluated criteria to determine which one has the least risk for you.
- If funds permit, consider putting refinance deals in place for as many qualified properties / tenants as you can afford, and start building your investment property portfolio

Step 4

Purchase the Property

At this point, you have secured your investment funds and you have identified your team of experts. Perhaps you've even started pulling your business together with a home office. And, most importantly now, you have identified a property and tenants that qualify with your selection criteria. Now, you're ready to move forward and purchase that home!

This is the most administratively challenging aspect of the entire lease option refinance system. You likely already know how much paper and details you need to manage when you purchase a home. Now, it's going to be even more because you also have to add in the lease option agreements, comprising the Occupancy Agreement, the Purchase Option Agreement, and various letters of direction for the lawyers to sort through.

You will also need to arrange for an appraisal (if it hasn't already been done) and a house inspection, and you will need to secure your mortgage for this property. Then, there will be all kinds of documents going back and forth as you get closer to the closing day.

Papers to sign with your lawyer and your bank and your insurance broker and so on.

Keeping track of all these things can be a real nightmare. Fortunately, I have included here for your use a checklist and timeline of the most important things that need to get done and when, so all you have to do is follow along to make sure you're on track.

Timeframe

One thing you will consistently come across in this strategy are tenants who are in a panic because their bank is going to foreclose on their property in a couple of weeks. It is, indeed, human nature to leave everything to the last minute, hoping that some miracle will present itself. The reality is, you cannot let their timetable highjack yours. You will need 4 – 6 weeks to complete the purchase transaction once you have qualified the tenant and the property, and once they have committed to the Lease Option Refinance Strategy.

So while it may be tempting to be the hero and push everyone to try to close a purchase in two weeks, the reality is you will simply annoy those partners you need: the mortgage lender, the mortgage broker, your lawyer, your insurance agent, and so on. Be clear on how much time this process will take: 4 – 6 weeks. And then stick to it.

Legal documents

You are already aware that you will need an agreement of purchase and sale for the property that you're about to invest in. But you may not be aware that this is the same time where you need to have your other agreements in place too, that is, the Occupancy Agreement, the Purchase Option Agreement, and the Letter of Direction for the tenant's lawyer.

Let's look at these documents separately.

Purchase and Sale Agreement

Depending on which jurisdiction the investment property is located in, the purchase and sale agreement may vary from place to place. Essentially, however, it is a contract that requires both parties to agree on the purchase price, the closing date, and what's included in the deal.

In this section, we'll consider each of these things separately, and we'll also cover off what conditions you are going to put into the agreement.

Determining your purchase price

This is, perhaps, the most important aspect of the transaction and one that can often lead to some confusion. Remember, the Lease Option Refinance Strategy is not a "vulture" type of strategy where you're going to swoop in and take advantage of someone's financial situation in order to purchase their home well below market value. We are going to offer the appraised value of the home, or slightly below the appraised value.

There are two reasons for this. First, it is only fair to the tenant that you would pay what the property is worth. Second, the tenant is going to need as much equity from his home as possible in order to pay out his debts, pay your commission, and have sufficient funds for his purchase option (which, as you know, is your 12 months of security).

If there is no recent appraisal on the property, this will need to get done quickly. You may choose to go ahead and put your offer to purchase in based on a best estimate, but both parties should realize that you will modify the purchase price based on an appraisal. Moreover, some lenders insist on doing their own appraisals anyway, and that can alter the purchase price too.

Since you will be working with a mortgage broker on your lease option refinance deals, the chances are pretty good that an appraisal will already have been ordered and performed. And just in case there is ever any question about it, the tenant pays for the appraisal, not you.

I often get asked whether the investor should offer, say, 5% less than the appraised value. That is certainly possible, since you are presumably the only buyer willing to help out the tenant. But keep this in mind. You will be receiving from the tenant a 5% commission on closing. That's what they would have to pay a real estate agent if they sold it on the market. Now if you want to reduce the purchase price by 5% or even 10%, that's starting to look a bit greedy to the tenant, and vulture-like. Not a great way to build a three year relationship with them. In my own dealings, I have always offered the full appraised value of a property.

The deposit

If you were buying a house for your own personal use, you know that you need to put a deposit on it as a show of good will and intentions. Usually, this deposit is held by the real estate agent or the seller's lawyer and, if the deal falls through, it is returned to you. If the deal goes ahead, the deposit is credited to your purchase.

In this case, we are not dealing with real estate agents. We are dealing directly with the seller. So the amount of the deposit does not have to be substantial. I have never had a deposit of more than $500 on any purchase. Often, I will only put in $100.

There's something else to consider as well. When the offer is accepted and you are required to actually send this deposit somewhere, the only person you will send it to is your own lawyer, in trust. Not the tenant's lawyer. Why is that? Simply because if the deal does not go through, you may have trouble getting your deposit back from someone other than your own lawyer.

The closing date

The closing date is the day when everything comes together and the title of the property changes hands from the tenant to you. It is a busy day for the lawyers and the bankers, and there may be last minute things to clarify. Quite often, the closing day itself may get pushed out and delayed because of things that come up. You can reduce the possibility of this happening by being prepared up front and by giving yourself sufficient time (4 – 6 weeks).

I'm going to say this part again because it's really important and you will be under a lot of pressure to close in 5 days or 2 weeks or whatever the panic number is. Don't do it. Don't make this your issue. You need 4 – 6 weeks to close a deal once all of the documents have been signed. Make sure your broker understands this so she can relay it to potential tenants.

I can tell you that in my early investing days when I was trying to be a hero to people, I would agree to close in two weeks only to annoy and frustrate everyone else that I needed to make the transaction go through smoothly. Lenders will not be pushed. Lawyers will not be pushed. House inspectors and appraisers will do their best to accommodate you, but that's not always possible. What happens is I ended up annoying my team and putting undue stress on me and my family. And for what? No other reason than I made someone else's problem my own. Let's avoid that kind of thing.

So, when you're filling in the closing date, you will need to consult with the tenant on this one. You will ask them how quickly they will be able to sign and return your offer to purchase. Chances are, they will take at least a couple of days, so in your own mind, you're thinking of a closing date that is now 5 – 7 weeks out. Moreover, they will also need to sign the Occupancy Agreement and the Purchase Option Agreement and the Letter of Direction before your offer becomes firm. These will take more time to review, because we want the tenants to obtain independent legal advice on these agreements so they understand exactly what they are committing to. This will add another week or two to the process.

So you can see how quickly the time builds up. Again, you will want to close 4 – 6 weeks from the time all of these documents have been signed, so it's important to get the tenants to focus on these things. Your mortgage broker can help in this regard too, since the broker really is the key person who has been working with the tenant to find a mortgage solution, and usually knows their situation better than most.

One thing you can do before you even get to the offer to purchase, is to provide the tenants with a draft copy of the Occupancy Agreement and Purchase Option Agreement early in your discussions so they can review them and perhaps even have their lawyer review them too. This will save considerable time and will also help guide the tenant's decision about going with your solution before too much time and effort are expended.

Let's assume now that your tenant is committed to get these documents reviewed and signed within a few days, so you are confident that you'll be able to close in 5 weeks. Have a look at the calendar and choose any day of the week as long as it isn't Friday. I find that either Tuesday or Wednesday is a good day to close. Why not Friday? Here's the thing. If you are choosing a Friday near the end of the month, that's generally the time when everyone else is closing and you may run into delays. If your purchase does not close on the Friday, then it won't close until the next week... probably Tuesday. So you're already several days behind in your transaction. The other problem with closing on a Friday is that, even if everything goes smoothly, you usually won't receive your proceeds (i.e., your commission, first and last month's occupancy payments, and the purchase option amount) until Monday or Tuesday of the following week. Maybe not a big deal, but for me, cash is always king and I want to see that cash in my account as quickly as possible.

So try to choose a Tuesday or Wednesday, not near the end of the month, for a closing day.

What's included in the purchase

To be clear with your tenants, you are buying their property and will be the owner of it. This includes things like appliances. So in your offer to purchase, you will make sure that the appliances are included in the deal and in case your tenants ask (some will), you are not paying anything extra for them.

This is yet another way to minimize your risks. If we suppose that your tenants are not able to complete their refinance term and are evicted, and that you now have to sell that home, you want to make it as attractive as possible for other buyers. Keeping the appliances in the deal is always helpful because then your property is in "move in condition".

Conditional Clauses

Your offer to purchase is going to be conditional on three things: your ability to obtain a new first mortgage, your ability to secure home insurance, and your satisfaction with a home inspection. These conditions are critical, and no matter how much pressure you may under to NOT include them, just say no. They will be in your offer to purchase, no ifs ands or buts.

Let's look at obtaining a new first mortgage. Even if you have been pre-approved for a mortgage of a certain amount, that really means absolutely nothing because when it comes time to actually secure a mortgage commitment from the bank, the bank will look at the specific property you want to purchase. It is no longer "theory".

Step 4 – Purchase the Property

Too often I've seen investors and other home buyers claim they have been pre-approved for a mortgage of a certain amount, only to find out that they can't get a mortgage for a specific property they want to buy. Very frustrating for all.

So this condition is important, and it looks like this:

The Offer is conditional upon the Buyer arranging, at the Buyer's own expense, a new first mortgage satisfactory to the Buyer in the Buyer's sole and absolute discretion. Unless the Buyer gives notice in writing delivered to the Seller not later than 15 business days from the date of acceptance that this condition is fulfilled, this Offer shall be null and void and the deposit shall be returned to the Buyer in full without deduction. This condition is included for the benefit of the Buyer and may be waived at the Buyer's sole option by notice in writing to the Seller within the time period stated herein.

Your lawyer may suggest other wording, but the idea behind this is the same: if you cannot arrange for a new first mortgage on the property, then the deal is dead.

The next condition is similar and it relates to obtaining home insurance on the property. For this insurance, we're only talking about the building itself, not the contents. The tenant's will need to get their insurance for their stuff, but you will need insurance on the building for things like fires. Again, the clause looks like this:

The Offer is conditional upon the Buyer arranging, at the Buyer's own expense, satisfactory insurance to the Buyer in the Buyer's sole and absolute discretion. Unless the Buyer gives notice in writing delivered to the Seller not later than 15 business days from the date of acceptance that this condition is fulfilled, this Offer shall be null and void and the deposit shall be returned to the Buyer in full without deduction. This condition is included for the benefit of the Buyer and may be waived at the Buyer's sole option by notice in writing to the Seller within the time period stated herein.

To secure your insurance on this property, you will need to provide your insurance agent with the following information:

- legal address of the property
- purchase price
- annual rental income
- specific details about the property itself, such as its effective age, number of rooms, type of heating and hydro, etc. Your insurance agent will have a list or form to fill out.

The third mandatory clause that you'll include in your offer is for a house inspection report that meets with your satisfaction. It will look like this:

The Offer is conditional upon the inspection of the subject property by a home inspector at the Seller's own expense, and the obtaining of a report satisfactory to the Buyer in the Buyer's sole and absolute discretion. Unless the Buyer gives notice in writing delivered to the Seller not later than 15 business days from the date of acceptance that this condition is fulfilled, this Offer shall be null and void and the deposit shall be returned to the Buyer in full without deduction. The Seller agrees to cooperate in providing access to the property for the purpose of this inspection on a timely basis. This condition is included for the benefit of the Buyer and may be waived at the Buyer's sole option by notice in writing to the Seller within the time period stated herein.

So what this means is that your offer is only going to be firm if you are satisfied with the condition of the property as evidenced by a house inspection report. I can't begin to tell you the number of times I have been saved by a house inspection. I remember one home I was looking at that had all kinds of mold and gross stuff in the attic. Another that had DIY wiring and was, quite simply, dangerous. Another with critter nests and so on. The house inspection will reveal all those things that you need to be aware of. It doesn't mean you won't go through with the purchase, but at least you and the tenant will have a better idea of what the property holds.

This clause also states that the seller, or tenant, will pay for this house inspection. You may be asked to pay for it yourself because the tenant may not have the cash to do it themselves. If you decide to pay for it, then the cost of the inspection will be reimbursed to you on closing.

Typically, the buyer will pay for things like an appraisal and a house inspection, but not when you are investing with the Lease Option Refinance Strategy. The reason for this is quite simple. If you were to make 10 offers on properties and none of them pass the house inspection to your satisfaction, you'll be out of pocket several thousand dollars. So the tenant will pay for this.

Signatures

The last thing I'm going to mention about the offer to purchase is signatures. Typically, when you sign your offer, there will be a place on the contract for a witness to sign as well. Do not ignore this, thinking that it's unimportant. I've had deals get hung up on closing day because the lender wanted to see my signature witnessed. It may seem a bit crazy, but that's the way it is. So, when you make your offer to purchase and sign it, have someone else put their signature on it as a witness. You'll save yourself a hassle later on.

Before we leave the offer to purchase, one other thing I like to do is to give my lawyer a "heads up" about the offer, so when it has been signed by the tenants, I forward a copy of the conditional offer to my lawyer just so he is aware of what's coming. He won't actually do any lawyer work on it until the offer is "firm".

If the property you're purchasing is in another jurisdiction (province or state), you will normally need a lawyer to handle the transaction who is in that jurisdiction. This adds another dimension to the purchase, but nothing overly burdensome. Your own lawyer can usually recommend someone or know how to find someone who will manage the transaction on your behalf. It will then be up to make sure that lawyer knows what you are doing and what to expect. That is, you will want to tell him that this is a lease option refinance, and that along with the offer to purchase, there will also be an Occupancy and Purchase Option Agreement, along with a letter of direction.

Occupancy Agreement

Now let's turn our attention to the Occupancy Agreement (OA). I invite you to follow along with OA template in the Appendix.

This agreement is like a rental agreement, but not quite, because it contains clauses that you generally won't find in a rental agreement. The OA outlines the terms and conditions of the three year refinance agreement, including who is responsible for what.

Let's have a look at the key clauses that you will need to fill out when you're putting this agreement together for a tenant. Remember, if you are unclear about any of these clauses, you should consult your lawyer. As well, each jurisdiction has different regulations, so the lawyer in the jurisdiction in which you're purchasing your property should review this agreement—and the Purchase Option Agreement—before you finalize them.

Preamble

In the first part of the agreement, the preamble shows who this agreement is between. That is, it is an agreement between you (the investor) and your tenants. There are a couple of things you want to keep in mind here. When it comes to the tenants, you want to include all of the adults in the property. Usually, this is the husband and wife. But it could also include granny or grampa or another adult. The reason for including all of the adults in the agreement is to—you guessed it—minimize your risk if something happens to one of them.

The preamble also has the full address of the property.

Throughout this agreement, you will notice that the word "tenant" does not appear. This is to differentiate between a "tenant" in a typical rental situation, and an "occupant" under the Lease Option Refinance Strategy. The occupant here is everyone who is listed in the preamble.

Clause 2

Next we're going to look at clause 2, which states:

In the space marked "Commencement Date", you will put the closing date for the purchase. This is the same one you used in the offer to purchase. If the closing date changes between the time the OA is signed and the actual day of closing, you will need to create an amendment to this agreement with the new commencement date.

What this date specifies is that the lease option refinance term begins on the same day as the purchase is closed.

The other thing to note is that the agreement is for 12 months only, but will be automatically renewed for up to a total of 36 months (3 years) if the tenant is in good standing. In other words, if the tenant is unable to maintain their obligations, you may terminate the OA. This protects you and will minimize your risks of carrying a three-year "lease" agreement if the tenant is less than ideal.

Clause 3

The third clause is critical, and is a key difference between the OA and a typical rental agreement. Here it is:

Notice the term "occupant" instead of "tenant" here. This clause is the one that the occupant will be very interested in because it shows that he will have a Purchase Option Agreement that will allow him to buy his property back at the end of the term. It also says that, if the occupant does not exercise this option, he will need to vacate. He will also forfeit his purchase option. We'll discuss this later.

Note here that we're also asking the occupant to initial this clause so that he shows his complete understanding and acceptance of it.

Clauses 4 and 5

These clauses stipulate how much the monthly occupancy fee (or "rent") will be, and what occupancy fees are owed you at the start of the OA (or, when you close the purchase of the property). You will need to enter the amount of the monthly fee in clause 4, along with the due date. For example, if you close your purchase of the property on June 12, then that becomes your due date for future occupancy fees.

You and your occupants may find it helpful to adjust the due date to the first of each month. If you do this, then you will need to cover the difference through the Letter of Direction to the lawyers.

In clause 5, you enter twice the monthly occupancy fee. One of these covers the first month of the OA, and the other covers the last month of the OA.

Clauses 6, 7, and 8

With these clauses, the penalties for late payments or missed payments are established. In clause 6, you are stating that if the occupant's monthly occupancy fee cheque is late or bounces, then there is an automatic $200.00 penalty. However, it also states that if the local jurisdiction does not allow penalties on late or missing rent, then the local jurisdiction laws shall prevail. In other words, the OA cannot override the laws of the land. As the owner, landlord and investor, you will need to check what the regulations are about this in the jurisdiction where the property that you're purchasing is. Your lawyer will be able to assist in this matter too.

Clause 7 states that if the monthly occupancy fee is late or missing, then you will reduce the purchase option by that amount. In other words, remember the 12 months of expenses you have put away in reserve? This is the occupant's payment for the right to purchase his home back, but it also serves as your security for things like missing payments. So if the monthly fee is late or missing, you will deduct it immediately from the reserve fund. When the occupant does make his payment, you will put it back into the purchase option / reserve fund. In this way, you will always have your monthly fee paid on time.

If the monthly occupancy fee is 5 days late, then the occupant is considered to be in breach of the agreement. This is very serious, because what it means is that you can legally terminate the OA and the Purchase Option Agreement, and evict the occupant and his family. And yes, he also forfeits his purchase option amount.

This is something that, in your early discussions with the occupant and with your mortgage broker, you will need to make extremely clear. The Lease Option Refinance Strategy is not for everyone. Occupants must appreciate the seriousness of the agreements and be willing to meet their obligations or else they will lose their home and their purchase option.

I find this really strange sometimes. A family will do everything they need in order to get into my Lease Option Refinance Strategy, and then before you know it, they are asking me not to cash their occupancy cheque or they just let it bounce and say "sorry" afterwards. When I was first starting out as an investor, I would tolerate this behaviour for a while, but then it just became a chronic problem. As a result, I don't do it now at all. If someone is late with their cheque or if their cheque bounces, then I immediately call the property manager and initiate the eviction process. It's amazing how quickly your occupants will take this process seriously when they miss a payment and the next day, the property manager shows up with an eviction notice.

Clauses 9 – 12

Have a look at these clauses. While there are fairly straightforward, I want to point out a couple of things. First is clause 9, which asks for the number of adults and children living in the property, and their names. This is important because it prevents your occupant, legally, from turning your property into a drop-in centre for all the assorted riff-raff of the world.

Your property, which you are allowing the occupant to live in, is only for them and no one else.

Clause 11 deals with pets, and often raises questions with the occupants. For example, if the family already owns a dog or cat, then it is assumed they will be able to keep Fido or Kitty while they are in the lease option refinance term. This is fine, as long as you know about it. Likewise, if the family wants to get a pet at some point during the term, they need your permission. Why? Because it is your property and you are the landlord. Pets can have a way of detracting from the value of a property, what with the hair and smell and poop in the back yard. You don't want to increase the risk of not being able to sell the property quickly if you need to. So, if the occupant wants a pet, they need your permission.

This clause also allows you the opportunity to put the brakes on exotic pets like snakes and ferrets and other critters. Just say "no" if someone wants a pet snake. If you have any doubts, the answer is always no.

Clause 13

This clause is concerned with maintenance of the property and who pays for it. Essentially, the occupant is agreeing on the condition of the property, and that he won't make any alterations to it without your permission.

Some occupants have a bit of difficulty with this because it has been their home and in the past, they were able to paint a room or replace a carpet whenever they wanted to. Now they have to ask your permission to do that. It's a bit of an adjustment for them, but as long as you are clear at the outset and during the refinance term, you shouldn't have any trouble managing this aspect of the agreement.

Clause 14

The same thing is true for clause 14. This clause makes it very clear that the occupant is responsible for things like plugged toilets and squeaky door hinges and so on… not you. These are some of the really annoying things you might encounter if you were the landlord of a long-term rental property. I've had some tenants call me about problems with their heating, water, toilets, wood fireplace, driveway cracks, leaf clean up… you name it. One of the greatest benefits of the Lease Option Refinance Strategy is that the occupant takes care of all these things as if they were still the owners. This reduces the burden on you for ongoing maintenance, as well as the property management fee since they won't have as much to do.

Clauses 15, 16, and 17

These clauses are fairly straightforward and cover things such as liability in the case of damage to the property and so on. If you have any questions about these, your lawyer will be able to clarify them for you.

Clause 18

If there is a fire and the property is damaged, and it is not the occupant's fault, then this clause brings some common sense into the picture. In your judgment—and only yours counts—if it will take too long to repair the property, then you can terminate the OA and return the occupant's purchase option funds. This might be the case, for example, if a fire destroyed the entire home and the only thing you could do is rebuild it. In this case, your insurance company would cover the cost of building the new home and, once built, you could then sell it.

Clause 19

This important clause reflects on what constitutes "default" under the agreement. Essentially, if all payments are not made, or if any of the terms of the agreement are not met, then the occupant is considered to be in default, and he forfeits his purchase option and is evicted. As well, if the occupant is absent from the property for 5 or more days while in default, then he is considered to have abandoned the property and forfeited his purchase option.

Again, the occupant's lawyer will be able to discuss the significance of this clause to the occupant, but you will also want to make sure it is clear to him, as well as to your mortgage broker who often gets these kinds of questions directly.

Clauses 20 – 33

The remainder of the OA covers additional liability items and related issues. They are designed to protect you from being sued for any reason if the occupant fails to meet his obligations under the agreement and is forced to vacate the premises and forfeit his purchase option.

This is as good a time as any to discuss possible legal action. If your occupant is forced out and loses his purchase option, he not only loses his home, but he is also out tens of thousands of dollars. This is strong incentive for him to want to sue you to try to recover some funds and to keep his home. That's why we have these air-tight agreements in place: to protect you and minimize your risk.

Do these agreements guarantee that you won't ever get sued? Of course not. But they will do two things. First, if the occupant seeks legal advice on whether he can sue or not, there won't be too many lawyers who would support action because the agreements are so solid. Second, if a lawyer ever did try to make up a case against you, it would be extremely difficult for him to win.

That's not to say that you can expect to get sued by an occupant if something goes wrong. The chances of that happening are very slim, but it is still important to be prepared for such an event just in case. When you take these agreements to your own lawyer for her opinion on them and to make sure they will work in the jurisdiction where you're investing, you can discuss the prospects of being sued at some point and determine for yourself whether this is a likely scenario or not. Some people and some jurisdictions are more litigious than others.

Now let's turn our attention to the other key agreement: the Purchase Option Agreement.

Purchase Option Agreement

The OA is only the first half of the key documents that your occupant will need to understand and agree to in order to be accepted into your Lease Option Refinance Strategy. The second half is the Purchase Option Agreement (POA).

A POA template is also shown in the appendix, so you can review that and follow along with this section.

Preamble

The preamble for the POA is almost the same as that for the OA. Note, however, the differences in terminology being used now. In the POA, you are no longer the "owner". Instead, you are now the "optionor", that is, you are the one offering an option to purchase. The occupant is now considered to be the "optionee". He is the one who is paying for the option to purchase.

The POA is also an agreement that needs to be signed up front along with the OA and the offer to purchase. It is part of a package of documents that you will need your client to sign before anything can take place.

Let's review the clauses.

Clause 1

This clause makes it very clear that you are offering the optionee i.e., the occupant, an option to purchase the property. Naturally, the optionee must be in good standing and both the OA and POA need to be met before this option can be offered. Otherwise, the optionee forfeits his option to purchase.

Clause 2

This is where you put the agreed-to repurchase price. Remember when you used the Cardinal Home Investments Financial Analyzer to determine whether your client could qualify for the Lease Option Refinance Strategy? In that analyzer, you determined what the repurchase price was going to be, based on an assumed annual market appreciation.

So you need to put that number in this clause.

Clause 3

Here we go with the big clause! This is the key one in the POA where the actual amount of the **option payment credit** is entered. Please note that we sometimes refer to this payment by many names, but it is the payment that you receive when you purchase the property, and comprises a sufficient amount to cover at least 12 months of expenses. This is also the payment that the occupant will forfeit if he does not successfully meet the terms and obligations of the Lease Option Refinance Strategy.

The Financial Analyzer shows you how much this amount is for 12 months. That is the default number of months in the spreadsheet. However, you may certainly increase this if there is plenty of equity in the home, and, the higher this is, the less risk you have.

Again, we are asking the optionee to initial this clause to show his understanding and acceptance of it.

Clause 4

Chances are, when you receive the option payment credit when you close the purchase of the property, you will simply put it in a regular savings or chequing account. Any interest accrued on this payment over the three year refinance term will also be credited to the occupant/optionee. This is only fair. It also points to the necessity of having a separate bank account for this fund, and to keep all bank statements and good records so that you can show not only the optionee but also your bookkeeper and accountant any transactions that may have taken place with this account.

Although the clause says that the option payment credit can be used any way you want to use it once you have received it, it is a good idea not to use it for anything other than a reserve fund. Here's why. Towards the end of the refinance term, the occupant will be preparing to secure his own new mortgage commitment (we assume that by this time, his finances are back on track). One thing virtually all lenders want to see is proof that a buyer has a sufficient down payment and funds to cover the closing costs. If you have kept this option payment credit in a separate bank account that also shows the occupant's name on it (more on this later), then the occupant will be able to show that they have the necessary funds to purchase the home back. If all the occupant has is a credit voucher or an offer to purchase with a large deposit on it, that's usually not good enough for a lender these days.

So, while you may be able to do some things with the option payment credit / reserve fund, the point of keeping this fund intact and separate from other transactions is so that you can use it in case of emergency, and for the occupant to demonstrate they have the funds to buy their home back at the end of the refinance term.

Clauses 5 and 6

Often, you will have clients ask whether they can buy their homes back before the end of the three year term. Since we want them to buy their homes back, then this is a desirable thing; however, we also need them in the term for at least a couple of years so there is some equity built up. As such, these clauses state that the option to purchase the home back may be exercised any time after 24 months. In my experience, it normally takes at least that long—usually longer—for a client to get their finances back in shape.

In addition, because the occupant is leaving the term early, which will create some additional costs for you, clause 6 states that there is an administrative fee of $1500 if the occupant exercises the option early.

Clauses 7 - 10

These clauses discuss the timeframes for exercising the option, and where the option itself must be sent.

Clause 11

If the occupant finds that he needs a little more time in order to secure his new mortgage, he may extend the terms and conditions of the OA and the POA for an additional 12 months, for a fee of $500.00. This situation can arise, for example, if the occupant has undergone a bankruptcy or consumer proposal of some sort, and lenders aren't quite ready to commit a new mortgage but indicate that they will be shortly.

If this is exercised, you simply extend your agreements by however long the occupant needs, up to 12 additional months.

Clause 12

This clause says that the closing date of the repurchase shall not be longer than 60 days. Ideally, what you want is the closing date for the occupant's repurchase to be on the last day of the OA term. So for example, if your OA is set to terminate on June 30, 2017, then that would be the day you want to close the sale of the property back to the occupant.

Clause 13, 14, and 15

Again, the optionee / occupant is reminded of his obligations under this agreement and under the OA. If there is any kind of termination of these agreements, the optionee will be in default and will forfeit his option payment credit.

Clause 16

When discussing the Lease Option Refinance Strategy with mortgage brokers and others, they often wonder whether the clients should be getting legal advice on these agreements and on the strategy itself. The answer is a resounding YES! We encourage clients to obtain independent legal advice on these agreements. We want them to feel assured with the knowledge that they have a solid understanding of what these agreements say and what their obligations are when they sign them.

So this clause says that the optionee has obtained independent legal advice, or at least has waived the right to obtain such advice.

Clauses 17 – 23

The remainder of the agreement contains general clauses that should be fairly straightforward. If you have any questions about any of these clauses, you should consult with your lawyer.

The last part of the POA is the signature page. You will note there is a place for the optionee / occupant signature and witnesses. Just like a lender, you will not accept this agreement unless the optionee's signatures are witnessed.

Letters of Direction

The Letter of Direction is the final document that you will need to get signed up front before you can finalize the purchase of the client's property. A letter of direction is a letter that directs the client's lawyer what to do on closing. You need to get it signed by the client and sent to his lawyer as soon as possible, otherwise, you will not receive any proceeds on closing.

I have included a template of the letter of direction in the appendix for your information.

You will note that this letter tells the client's lawyer that you will be expecting three (3) separate financial items on closing. They are:

- your fee of 5% of the purchase price
- the first and last month's occupancy fee, as per the OA
- the option payment credit, as per the POA

You may also have additional expenses that you would collect here as well. For example, if you paid for the house inspection instead of the client, then you would recover your cost here. Same thing if you paid for an appraisal. Remember, you should not pay for these things out of your pocket: it is the client's responsibility.

Part of the letter of direction stipulates what the client's lawyer is to do with these funds. He is directed to pay them to your lawyer. He should not pay them directly to you or anyone else other than your lawyer. This will take place on the day of closing.

The letter of direction, therefore, needs to be signed by your client and sent to his lawyer. You will also want to get a copy of the signed letter of direction too, and you will send a copy of that to your lawyer. The reason being is that, when the lawyers are talking about the transaction, they are both aware of the letter of direction and if there's any problem with it on the client's end, your lawyer will be in a position to protect your interests.

So there we have it! Four key documents:
- Agreement of Purchase and Sale
- Occupancy Agreement
- Purchase Option Agreement
- Letter of Direction

Now one thing you'll have to keep in mind is that there's a strong possibility that some of the numbers could change. For example, if you don't have an appraisal done, or if your lender wants a new appraisal, then that could change your offer to purchase which will subsequently affect the numbers in the other documents. Therefore, be prepared to amend these documents as you go along. That doesn't mean you need to redo them all. But you will need to prepare a letter of amendment for each one, replacing the "old" numbers with the "new" numbers.

I'll tell you right now, the paper burden around these transactions can be massive, and keeping track of each version of each agreement can be a real challenge. That's why I make sure to include a version number in the filename for each one. I also create a folder with the final paper versions in it for future reference and in case my computer crashes.

Setting Up Bank Accounts

I have mentioned bank accounts a few times in this strategy so far, and now I'd like to expand on them. As you know, keeping track of all the transactions that take place in an active investment like this is critical. Your bookkeeper and accountant need to know precisely what your business is all about, and the tax department will be thankful too! Moreover, you'll appreciate keeping your accounts in order so you can track your investment and related expenses closely.

Here's what you'll want to do. Set up two bank accounts for your investment property. The first account is going to be your "operations" account. This is a chequing account where your mortgage and tax payments will come out of, along with property management fees (if any), insurance payments, and any other expenses related to the property. The second account is your reserve fund. This is where you will keep your occupant's option payment credit, and you could make it a regular savings account. Because there will be a significant amount of cash in this account, you will likely earn a bit of interest on it over the course of the refinance term. This interest is passed on to the occupant at the end of the term.

Now here's something that you'll need to be aware of with this reserve account. It is important to make sure that the occupant's name is also on the account. This doesn't mean that the occupant will have any kind of access to the account…he won't. But when the occupant goes to secure a mortgage commitment when he buys back the property from you, his lender will want to see proof that he has sufficient funds for the down payment and closing costs. They will want to see his name attached to an account with those funds in it. Your mortgage broker will be able to provide current advice on this matter, and you can always check with your bank or your lawyer about setting up this account so that your occupant's name appears on it even though they won't have any authority to withdraw those funds.

Monthly Occupancy Fees

These "fees" are better known to most people as "rent". Just as renters must pay their rent every month, your occupants will need to pay their occupancy fee every month. What you'll want to do is collect post-dated cheques up front for the entire term. These will need to be given to you before the purchase closes.

Why cheques and not electronic transfer? Because with cheques, you have a paper trail in case you ever need to show the cheque going in your account, and then bouncing. It is in your best interest to collect post-dated cheques from your occupants as part of the purchase closing process.

Some occupants will tell you that they'll give you 12 cheques now and the rest later. That is not acceptable. Remember, you want to minimize your effort here, and I can tell you that when I have allowed some occupants to only give me half a year or one year's worth of cheques, I inevitably end up having to email them, phone them, and generally push them when new cheques are needed. You don't want that hassle, so be sure to collect all the cheques for the entire term up front.

Managing the Reserve Fund

Speaking of the reserve fund, let's talk about how to manage these funds. Remember, the POA says that you have unfettered use of these funds, which means that you can do with them what you please. But be careful. This is not free money. It is returned to or credited back to the occupant when he purchases his property from you at the end of the refinance term. However, most lenders these days do not accept a "credit". They need to see the cold, hard cash sitting in an account with your occupant's name on it. As well you will need access to these funds in case the occupant is late with his monthly occupancy fee, or needs to be evicted. So this reserve fund needs to be managed wisely.

The occupant may also be a little leery of you keeping all that cash that he has given you. While it may not be an issue for the tenant, I feel the best thing you can do is to leave these funds in trust with your lawyer. By doing that, you make it clear to the tenant that you will not be using these funds for anything other than their intended purpose. It adds an additional element to the process, but nothing that you can't arrange fairly easily, and it builds a lot of trust with your tenant, lenders, brokers and lawyers.

Whether it's you managing this fund or a lawyer managing it, the conditions for taking money out of it are the same. You don't want to be using this account to fund anything other than what is needed for your investment property. That keeps the fund transactions separated from any of your personal affairs, which is what you want.

Here are the key conditions when you will want to access the fund. You can discuss this with your occupant and even put it in writing if he insists. In my experience, most occupants are not that concerned with the fund management.

So, you will withdraw cash from this reserve fund when:
- the occupant's monthly occupancy cheque bounces
- the occupant's monthly occupancy fee is late

- the occupant needs to be evicted
- after the occupant has defaulted and left the premises, so you can fix up the property and sell it

There may be other occasions in your particular circumstance where you will want to have access to this fund. As long as you are clear on what these conditions are, and as long as they are reasonable expenses related to the ongoing management of the property, you should not have any issues.

Finally, when you're shopping around for an account for this fund, be sure to see which ones waive the monthly bank fee if there is a minimum balance in it. You will save a good chunk of cash over the 36 month term this way.

Well, we have covered a lot of material in this section! You'll want to go through this information a few times so that you understand all the different moving parts involved in a lease option refinance transaction. If you do have any questions about this, or require assistance with your lease option refinance scenario, please contact me at david@cardinalhomeinvestments.com and I will be happy to assist.

Step 4 Highlights

- The legal arrangement between you and your tenant is secured by an Occupancy Agreement and a Purchase Option Agreement. As with any legal document, please ensure these are reviewed by your lawyer and, where necessary, modified to reflect the requirements in your own jurisdiction.
- The Agreement of Purchase and Sale, and the Letters of Direction are also important documents that will be completed by you during the process.
- Other requirements to complete as you set up your investment are bank accounts and managing your reserve fund.

Step 5

Manage the Property

In this step, you are now the owner of an income property. Your occupants are in the home. You have been paid your up front fee, option payment credit, and first and last month's occupancy fees. You are now ready to manage the property.

As I've mentioned already in this book, one of the key benefits of having the previous homeowner as your occupant in the 7 Step Lease Option Refinance Strategy is that he is already used to taking care of his home, and he will continue to do that. The Occupancy Agreement details all of the specific things that you and the occupant are responsible for, but to summarize, the only things you are responsible for are paying the mortgage, property tax, and building insurance. On the other hand, your occupant is responsible for all of the maintenance.

This is unlike a typical long-term rental situation where the landlord is responsible for things like fixing the furnace or repairing holes in the wall or unplugging the toilet. In the 7-Step Lease Option Refinance Strategy, the occupant is responsible for all these things. He takes care of them as if he was still the owner. That's really important for you, because you don't want to be a traditional landlord, right? If you did, you would be buying homes and renting them out long-term instead of looking at this strategy.

The other incentive for your occupant to look after the home herself is that she knows she will be buying the home back from you at the end of the three year term. With that being the case, it is in her best interest to keep the home maintained and looking nice.

So in terms of managing the property, and the occupants, there is only one real thing you need to concern yourself with: ensuring the monthly occupancy fees are paid and the cheques don't bounce.

Let's take a look at what that monthly occupancy fee covers.

Monthly expenses

As you can see from the Financial Analyzer, there are certain things you need to pay every month as the owner of the property. You will also note that the monthly occupancy fee is determined not by some magical number, but from the actual expenses. In other words, the occupant pays a fee based on these actual expenses and nothing more.

There are five items that the monthly occupancy fee must cover:
- your mortgage payment
- property taxes
- insurance
- your monthly return
- property management fees

Let's consider these separately.

Mortgage payment

When you are first discussing the Lease Option Refinance Strategy with your client (or with the mortgage broker, for that matter), you may need to estimate some of these costs. The mortgage payment is straightforward. You plug in the mortgage rate and the monthly payment is provided to you. And just to be clear, you are calculating the principle plus interest here.

Some lenders offer to collect and pay the property taxes as well. If your lender is offering this, take them up on it because it reduces the amount of work and tracking you actually need to do. Some of my lenders are doing this for me, others are not, and I can tell you that for those properties where taxes are paid as part of the mortgage payment are way easier to manage.

Property taxes

On property taxes, you should already know what the current taxes are from the documents you received from the broker. To estimate this, take the annual taxes and add an additional 10% to it. Then divide this amount by 12 to get the monthly amount. Because you the monthly occupancy fee is fixed over the three year term, and property taxes will inevitably go up during that time, you need to estimate what the average monthly fee would be over those 36 months.

Insurance

The insurance cost doesn't normally increase, so I have found it okay just to take the monthly fee from the insurance company and add it in. Many insurance brokers will offer a monthly payment plan instead of paying the insurance all at one time. There is usually a cost associated with this option, but it isn't very much and I recommend you take this option. When you pay things on a monthly basis, it's just a lot easier to manage things. You see the monthly occupancy fee go into your account, and you see the trackable expenses go out of your account.

Your monthly return

Now we get to the fun stuff! You will recall that in the Lease Option Refinance Strategy, you earn money three ways: at the beginning of the refinance term when you collect your 5% fee, at the end of the refinance term when you get the proceeds of sale, and every month during the refinance term.

Typically, I add an annual return of 12% to the cost of the refinance. This becomes a monthly return which is covered by your occupant. So in this way, your occupant is paying you your monthly return. You make money every time you cash one of their cheques.

I use 12% as the annual rate because it seems to be just the right number. It means that if I'm borrowing my investment funds from my HELOC at 3.5% and I'm earning 12%, then my net gain is 8.5% before taking into account the tax advantage of using borrowed funds for investment purposes.

Could you use a healthy 8.5% return, paid out monthly? Compare that with some of your bank's income certificates or government bonds, and you'll see how powerful this Lease Option Refinance Strategy really is.

The additional benefit to you is as follows. Suppose your occupant is unable to meet his obligations and you evict him from the property after 12 months. No worries. You have already received your return for the year…cash in your pocket. It's not like you *need* him to complete the refinance term before you can make any money, although that's ultimately what we want. Like I said, every time you cash a cheque, you are putting cold hard cash in your pocket.

Property management

The number you put in here for property management will depend on how much you do yourself and how much you contract out. For example, if you decide to work with a professional property manager—something I recommend doing, by the way—then you will put their monthly fee in here.

Now, the only thing you really need the property manager to do on a regular monthly basis is to drive by the house, take some pictures, and do a quick walk-through. That's it. If you do need their services for things like an eviction, the cost of that will come from the occupant's option payment credit… your reserve fund. This is not an ongoing monthly expense.

So once you have determined these monthly expenses, you simply add them all up to determine what your occupant will need to pay as his monthly occupancy fee.

Paying for water

In some municipalities, the local authorities will not bill occupants or tenants directly. Instead, they will bill you because you are the legal owner. This is, without doubt, annoying for you. But it isn't brain surgery, so the thing to do is to ensure that the day you receive a water bill from the municipality, you scan it and send it to your occupant.

While this does make some more work for you, there is an advantage to you receiving the water bills. You can determine whether the occupants are actually paying their bills or not. This is like the old canary in the coal mine thing. If your occupants are not paying their water bill, you can bet they are also behind in their electric and heating bills too. And this means they are probably behind in their other financial obligations. This is important information to you because, remember, you want to sell this property back to them at the end of the refinance term. If they are not paying their bills on time now, it's probably accurate to say that they are not improving in their financial situation. This is definitely a red flag.

So what can you do? Well, you cannot force someone to seek credit counseling or anything like that, but you can remind them of the consequences of not getting their financial house in order: they will lose their home and their option payment credit. These are serious consequences.

Other than making sure you deposit the monthly occupancy cheques on the right day, the only other thing you will want to know is whether the occupants are actually looking after the home or not. You will achieve this assurance by having someone drive by the property every month, take a few pictures of it, and send them to you. This will give you a good indication as to whether the yard is being looked after. As well, whoever is taking these pictures will also do a once a month quick walk-through of the home. This will make sure that it also isn't a dump and that there aren't non-occupants living there.

This is easy to arrange. If the income property is in your community, then you could do it yourself. But if you want completely hands off, or if the income property is in a community other than yours, you can arrange to have someone do it on your behalf. This could either be a property manager, or you could simply put an ad in kijiji looking for someone who will do this, and pay them a few bucks every month to do it. I find that $50 is more than enough to have someone take some pictures and keep an eye on the place for you. Another option is to ask your mortgage broker who may also be in the same community as the occupant. Perhaps he knows someone who could use some extra cash… maybe a student or retiree, for example. The bottom line is, you need some assurance that your property is being looked after and that it isn't being taken over by a cult of hippies.

Professional property management

Notwithstanding the ongoing, monthly deposits and checkups of your property, there may be times when you will need to get more directly involved with the business of your home, or engage the services of a professional property manager.

Let's suppose that your occupants pull something like this. Their occupancy cheque bounces. Then you call them up about it. They give you a story about the car needing repairs, or the kid's soccer fees or whatever, and then send you a new cheque next week. And then let's suppose this goes on almost month after a month, so you are in fact never sure whether their occupancy cheque will bounce or not.

That's not a pleasant investment to manage, is it? If you're like me, you just want things to work. You don't want or need complications…even little ones like the odd bounced cheque. So my recommendation for all lease option refinance properties is to secure the services of a professional property manager so that you don't have to lose sleep over these things.

There's an old saying about to-do lists, and it's the 4-D approach to those items on it. For everything on your to-do list you can:

- Do it
- Dump it
- Delay it
- Delegate it

In the case of property management, my preference is always to delegate the function to a property manager. Why? Simply because they have the expertise to deal with all kinds of tenants that I don't have, and they also remove that burden from me. A good property manager is worth her weight in gold.

So when you're setting up your arrangement with your occupant, you should also be looking into the services of a local property manager. You should be able to find all kinds on the internet, so check each one out and determine which one is the most appropriate for what you need.

And what is it that you need? Let's be clear, this isn't like a typical property management service… one that will find tenants for you, screen them, chase after them for missed payments etc. No. You don't need all that. What you do need is someone who you can call whenever the occupant's cheque bounces or you need to evict the occupants.

Here's what you need from a property manager. First and foremost, the most important service you can obtain is eviction. You want to find a manager who is experienced in evicting deadbeats from properties. They need to understand all of the local regulations about evictions, all of the rules that need to be followed, all of the forms that need to be filled out, and so on. In most jurisdictions, the landlord-tenant rules are heavily biased towards the tenants, and this is an area that requires specific expertise that most of us don't have, nor wish to have. But an experienced property manager will know exactly what to do, and this expertise is vital in order to get a deadbeat occupant out of your property so you can sell it and move on.

So, the specific services that you want from a property is the following:
- following up on late or bounced occupancy payments
- eviction, if necessary

When discussing your needs with the property manager, you will need to be clear with them about what you are doing with the 7-Step Lease Option Refinance Strategy. They will probably want copies of the OA and POA for their records, so they know what to do and what the timeframes are. Other than that, you don't need anything else from them (unless, of course, you are also asking them to do the monthly check ins with your occupants).

The main point of using a property manager here is so that you don't have to get involved with the "messy" part of the business. If a cheque bounces or your monthly occupancy is otherwise not paid on time, all you want to do is make one phone call or send one email to your property manager and have him deal with it.

Meanwhile, you take the missing funds from the reserve fund to ensure that your expenses are paid. That's why you have the reserve fund: so you are never out of expenses.

Credit counseling

The reason why your occupants got into the mess they're in is because they missed some mortgage payments or credit card payments, ruined their credit rating, and couldn't get their mortgage renewed. It's not uncommon, as you know, and we're not judging how people got into this trouble. But we do want to make sure they are doing what they need to do in order to get out of this situation. So we buy their properties under the 7-Step Lease Option Refinance Strategy, and put them on the path to recovery.

However, one thing that often goes unnoticed is this business about repairing credit. Unless your occupants can get their credit repaired, they will not qualify for a new mortgage at the end of the refinance term, and you will get stuck with a house you don't need or want. So getting your occupants into a good credit counseling program is really important.

Let me share with you what I've done in the past about this. One thing I tried was to put a clause in the OA stipulating that a condition of the refinance was that they go to a credit counselor for tips and strategies that could help them. What happened was that they either ignored this (it is difficult to enforce) or they went to a couple of sessions, ignored the advice, and never went back. On other occasions, I have suggested credit counseling services, occupants have attended them, and they have taken the steps to improve their situation. So much depends on the individuals involved, and for someone who used to be a homeowner, telling them that they now need counseling is a tough prescription to follow.

So what can you do? In my agreements now, I do not put in any clauses about mandatory attendance at a credit counseling session. However, in my discussions with them, I do emphasize the importance of these sessions and mention how the most successful participants in the 7-Step Lease Option Refinance Strategy are those who attend credit counseling sessions. This seems to help them get going on the right path.

The other thing that helps is getting the occupant involved in credit counseling as soon as your purchase their property. That is, as soon as the term begins, they should be looking at building up their credit rating. I have found that occupants are most receptive to this at the beginning of the term. Once they have been in it for six months or so, they are accustomed to the new schedule and their focus shifts. So ideally what we want is for the occupant to get into a credit counseling program as soon as possible.

Annual credit report

Now you may have also noticed in the OA that you can ask for a credit report from your occupant every year. This is, of course, optional and totally up to you, but I can tell you that I have always asked for a copy of their credit report every 12 months. The purpose of this is to monitor how they are improving their credit score.

Some occupants will whine about this requirement. They will give you all kinds of excuses not to do it, such as "it costs too much", or "it will impact my credit score". Listen. I have heard all the excuses. But let's put this into perspective. You are handing over a $350,000 asset to strangers, and you are trusting that they will do what is needed so they will look after your property and buy it back from you at the end of the term. This is no small thing. And, in order to assuage your concerns that they will be able to meet their obligations at the end of the term, you have a right to know how they are moving towards improving their credit so that they'll be able to purchase their home back from you at the end of the refinance term.

Some occupants will give you a sob story in order to avoid this requirement. Do not fall for it. Remember, this is a business, not a charity. Your main focus is to make money and to avoid undue risk. If you start getting soft with their stories about dying puppies and youth sports fees and so on, you are doomed. Most importantly, if you are sensitive by nature and prone to sympathize with people by default, then you really do need to find a property manager who will take care of all these nasty things so you don't have to get personally involved.

Step 5 Highlights

- Calculation of the tenant's monthly occupancy fee is based on real monthly expenses, not on guesses.
- Within the monthly occupancy fee is your own monthly return
- Unless you are extremely comfortable with managing properties and tenants, I strongly recommend finding a solid property management firm with a good reputation to handle this aspec of ycur investment. Remember, this is about making money with minimal risk—not about becoming a property manager.

Step 6

Sell the Property

In this section, we're going to look at what happens at the end of the 7-Step Lease Option Refinance Strategy term when it's time to sell the property to the occupant.

A successful refinance here is one where the occupant has gotten his financial house in order, paid his monthly occupancy fee on time, and is ready to buy his home back from you. This is the best case scenario for everyone. So, as long as you have done your part and managed things well—either personally or through a property manager—and the occupant has done his part, then there should be no issues. That said, there are some things that are outside of your control, in particular, whether a lender will provide a mortgage commitment to your occupant.

Let's look at how things should unfold, starting at about 6 months before the end of the term.

Role of the mortgage broker

Remember the mortgage broker who found your client and helped put your deal together? Well he hasn't disappeared. In fact, he will have been keeping regular contact with the occupant to make sure that his credit is improving and that he's on track to get a new first mortgage. Now you may be thinking why the mortgage broker would be doing this extra unpaid work, but the reality is that it's a small price to pay for ensuring that the occupant will use his services to get himself a new mortgage.

So at about six months before the end of the term, the broker will begin the mortgage application process. He will collect the pertinent financial information from the occupant and will begin shopping around for the best terms and conditions. If the occupant's credit is still not quite good enough to get a decent mortgage commitment, he can always opt for an extension of the Occupancy Agreement, but for the purpose of demonstration here, let's suppose that his credit is good again and he can select the best mortgage available. But before he can get an actual commitment, as opposed to "pre-qualification", you will need to have a signed Agreement of Purchase and Sale between you and the occupant.

Offer to purchase

This offer will be very similar to the one you signed with the occupant before the start of the refinance term. Although this will have the occupant as the buyer and you as the seller, you will still need to prepare the document or at least provide the salient information to your occupant. Here, the offer will be for the agreed-to repurchase price as shown in the Purchase Option Agreement. In addition, the closing date will be the last day of the refinance term. There will be no conditions on this offer. In other words, the occupant is committed to buying the property back. Finally, and this is something that is quite important, the amount of the deposit that is listed on this offer to purchase is the entire amount of their option payment credit, plus any accrued interest.

The reason for including the entire amount of the option payment credit is to ensure that the occupant is committed to buying the property back from you. Remember, if the deal falls through once the offer is signed, and it is not your fault, the occupant/buyer will forfeit his deposit. You want to make sure that if there is a forfeit, then you will receive the entire amount of the option payment credit.

This is also the time where that reserve fund account comes into play. Recall that when you set it up, you put the occupant's name on the account. Now the broker can show the lenders that the occupant has the required down payment and closing costs covered, and there won't be any issues with trying to find it when it comes time to close the deal.

Okay, so the occupant obtains a mortgage commitment and is ready for the next step. You have a signed Agreement of Purchase and Sale with a closing date the same as the end of the refinance term. The other item that needs to be taken care of is actually exercising the option to purchase.

Exercising the option to purchase

Let's refer again to the Purchase Option Agreement template in the appendix. Clause 7 states:

> The Option shall be exercised by mailing or personally delivering written notice to the Owner sixty (60) days prior to the Expiration of the Option and by additional payment, on account of the purchase price, in the amount of [$X,XXX.XX] (the "Exercise of Option Fee") payable directly to the Owner.

What this means is that the occupant has to physically pay you a fee in order to exercise the option, and this payment must be sent to you 60 days before the end of the refinance term. The amount of the Exercise of Option Fee is the same as the monthly occupancy fee.

Remember that you have already collected a "last month's rent" fee at the beginning of the refinance term, so this may factor into the occupant's budgeting. For this reason, it is imperative that you maintain frequent contact with your occupant to ensure that he is aware of the obligations in the OA and POA, and that he is able to meet the requirements of exercising the option.

Closing the Sale

The only thing left to do now is to close the sale of the property back to the occupant. The lawyers, naturally, will be doing most of the paper work to close it. Your lawyer may ask you to transfer the purchase option credit to his firm, in trust, during the process. Or he may simply make adjustments for it. You can discuss this with him.

On the day of closing, or the next day, you will receive the proceeds of the sale comprising your original investment plus some additional profit on the sale. Your occupant is now the homeowner of his property again, his finances are back in order, and you have helped him keep his home and preserve most of the equity in it. In fact, if the actual housing market has appreciated more than what you estimated, then your homeowner will be extra happy because he bought his home back from you at a bargain.

He wins by getting his home back and preserving his equity. You win because you have had a solid investment experience with low risk and double digit returns.

Step 6 Highlights

- Your mortgage broker plays a key role in helping your tenants secure a new mortgage.
- The purchase option that the tenant provided to you at the start of the term is now used for their down payment and closing costs.
- There are a lot of little details to manage as you move towards completing the sale of the home back to the tenants. You will need to stay on top of them all!

Step 7

Do it Again!

Congratulations! You did it! You're probably thinking at this point that you never realized how much effort is required owning and managing income-generating real estate. But at the same time, you also know how rewarding it can be to see a family come to you with very little hope and completely stressed out to the max, and then in three short years, you have helped them solve their financial problem and get back on their feet and back into their old home.

It's my hope that you have now gained all the knowledge and expertise to take your business to the next level. That is, if you have kept all the profits you made from your first property, you can now take those profits and invest in even more. This is the way to build a small fortune in a relatively short period of time, and something we're going to look at more closely in this chapter.

Reinvest your profits

As we'll see in the next chapter when we run through all the numbers in a typical lease option refinance scenario, you will earn about $75,000 from your first investment property. If you borrow from your HELOC, you'll make a little less because you'll need to service your debt, but you'll also gain some tax advantages as well. And, if you rely on a property manager or if you partner up with Cardinal, then you'll have earned a little less too. But let's just say for the purpose of demonstration that you earn $75,000 so that the new total that you have to invest in another property is $175,000.

If you take another look at Chapter 5 where we calculated how much property we could buy with $100k, you'll see now that you're able to purchase up to:

Maximum property value = $175,000 / (0.25 + 0.03)

= $175,000 / 0.28

= $625,000

That's a lot of dough to leverage in the lease option refinance program, and you can see how quickly this can grow in a very short period time. The temptation, naturally, is to spend those returns as they come in and there's really nothing wrong with that. In fact, many retirees use this strategy as a way to supplement their income. But if your in your 20s, 30s, 40s or 50s, you can keep using this strategy for 10 or so years, reinvest your profits, and then retire and do this as your full-time occupation.

But let's return to our example above. Just because you can leverage $625k worth of property doesn't mean that you have to put it all into one property. In fact, you could probably purchase two properties with your profits from your first one.

This has certain advantages because you are minimizing your risk even more. If you have one property and the occupants bail on you, then you have to do some work to sell the place and, even though you have a nice reserve fund to fall back on, the point of this strategy is to find occupants that stay in their homes and complete their obligations. But if you have two or more properties and one of the occupants bails, you still have your other property chugging along, making you all kinds of money while you sell the one you need to.

So as you move forward with this strategy, keep the above in mind. Ultimately, what you're going to do is build a lease option refinance portfolio of properties.

If you continue to do this—reinvest your profits and keep buying up more income properties—then in a few short years, you will have generated at least one million dollars in profits. And most importantly, you will have created that wealth the smart way without taking on undue risks and without taking on all kinds of extra work.

So let's go through exactly how this strategy works by looking at all the numbers and calculations needed to turn an initial investment of $100k into at least $1,000,000.

Step 7 Highlights

- To turbocharge your wealth-building using the 7-Step Lease Option Refinance Strategy, all you need to do is reinvest your returns from your first investment into new investments.
- Over time a period of 10 years or so, by following this strategy, you should realize outstanding gains on your investments.

Chapter 5

A Typical Refinance Scenario: Making the Strategy Work in the Real World

No one has ever become poor by giving.

Anne Frank

In this chapter, we're going to crunch all the numbers and walk you through a typical lease option refinance scenario so you can see exactly how all the steps work together in a realistic example.

Our goal with this strategy is to build considerable wealth without taking on excessive risk and without having to do a whole lot of work. We understand that there's a fair bit to do up front, especially in pulling your documents together for your mortgage broker. But once that's done and you own your income property, you don't want to have to do any of the follow up with your occupants if at all possible. In other words, we're looking for double digit returns with minimal risk and minimal work.

So now we're going to walk through the entire process from the time you have purchased your lease option refinance property to the time you sell it. Our focus here is going to be on the numbers and understanding how they all work together.

Your first $350k purchase

With your investment cash of $100k, you're able to purchase a property valued at $350,000. For the purpose of demonstrating the numbers in the Lease Option Refinance Strategy, we're going to start with this purchase and, where possible, round off the numbers a bit to keep things simple. Please note that each individual scenario will be different your actual numbers will vary depending on things like your purchase price, your investment funds, the mortgage rates, your desired monthly rate of return, the market appreciation, and so on.

To understand all the numbers, let's take a close look at the Cardinal Home Investments Financial Analyzer spreadsheet. Here, we're going to focus on the first section relating to your purchase of the home.

Financial Analysis Lease Option Refinance Typical Scenario 3 Year Term			
	%	Monthly Figures	Actual Figures
Purchase Price			$350,000
Financing Information			
1st Mortgage	75%		$262,500
Total Mortgage			$262,500
Investment Required			
Downpayment	25%		$87,500
Closing costs	3.0%		$10,500
Total Investment	28.00%		$98,000

Figure 5-1. The Lease Option Purchase

The initial financial information is shown in Figure 5-1. Here, you can see that we have entered the purchase price of $350,000 and we're going to secure a first mortgage at 75% LTV. This means that we will need to come up with a down payment of 25% plus the closing costs. The closing costs here have been estimated at 3% of

A Typical Refinance Scenario: Make the Strategy Work in the Real World

the purchase price, but they will vary depending on the jurisdiction where the property is located, since some jurisdictions charge taxes or related fees that others don't. Your mortgage broker will be able to provide you with a conservative estimate for these costs.

So what we see here is a need to come up with $98,000 in order to purchase this $350,000 lease option refinance property.

In Figure 2, we're going to look more closely at the equity in the property and some of the fees associated with the Lease Option Refinance Strategy. In this example, we see that when the purchase of the property closes, the occupant is going to receive the proceeds of sale, that is, $350,000. This is what we see in the first line. We are also going to assume here the that occupant has outstanding debts of $200,000. These would include the mortgage that he's paying out, and any other consumer debts that he needs to get rid of. That's line 2. As such, the total amount of equity available to the occupant in the property is $150,000.

There are other fees that will need to be paid out too. For example, the occupant is going to need to pay for his lawyer to close the purchase and sale transaction, so those fees will come out of his equity. As well, the occupant needs to pay you your fee, which is 5% of the purchase price, or $17,500 in this example. This fee goes into your pocket for the efforts and expertise you bring to the lease option refinance transaction. Depending on where you live, you may need to pay taxes on this too. If you do, then the taxes you pay will also be collected from the occupant's equity: you will not be paying those taxes out of your commission. Check with your lawyer to see how to handle any tax implications of this commission.

Funds from client's equity		
Client Proceeds from sale		$350,000
Client Mortgage/Debt Payouts		($200,000)
Equity Before Fees		**$150,000**
Client's legal costs to sell		($1,500)
Investor Fee from client's equity	5.00%	($17,500)
Less: Broker referral fee	$500	($500)
First and Last month's occupancy fees		($5,368)
Equity Available Before Referral Fees		**$125,132**
Less: Reserve Funds Required (in months)	12	($32,209)
Purchase Option Amount		**$32,209**

Figure 5-2: The Lease Option Occupant Funds

The next line you see in Figure 5-2 is the "Broker referral fee". This is the $500 you provide to the mortgage broker who brings the potential client to you in the first place, and who collects all of the up front documentation that you'll need for your due diligence. I like to put in place a letter of understanding with brokers around this. It doesn't have to be overly formal, but it's always good to have clarity around these things as to who is responsible for what. For example, in the Lease Option Refinance Strategy, the mortgage broker is expected to refer a potential client to you along with all of the documents they would normally collect in their mortgage application. Chances are, the broker has already collected these documents because they've tried to find a new lender for this client, so it should not add any additional work for them. A quick email or letter saying that you agree to pay the broker $500 for a referral that becomes an occupant, along with all the salient documents, should suffice. You should also stipulate that the broker will get paid upon successful closing of the purchase. In other words, if the deal falls apart and does not close, then you don't pay the broker at all.

The next line comprises two months of occupancy fees that we refer to as "first and last month's". These fees come directly out of the equity of the property. It means that you will collect, on closing, two months of occupancy fees. The number used here comes from the monthly cash flow in Figure 3. More on that in a second.

We now subtract those above fees from the equity in the property and arrive at the next line which is the "equity available before the option payment credit". For many clients, this is the moment of truth because if they don't have sufficient equity in their homes to cover off 12 months of expenses in the form of an option payment credit, then they simply do not qualify for the Lease Option Refinance Strategy.

Let's talk about the 12 months of expenses being held as the option payment credit. Some investors have asked me whether this much coverage is too much…that is, could we only collect 3 or 4 months worth of expenses? My response to this is an emphatic NO. In my experience, and depending on the jurisdiction, it can take at least 6 months to evict a deadbeat tenant, and when they do leave, you will likely have to spend some money to get the place repaired well enough to sell.

So in fact, 12 months is the minimum I would ever collect. And if there is anything about the occupants of the property that I think is even a tiny bit risky, I will increase that to 18 months to be on the safe side. That way if anything ever did go wrong, it's not my investment cash at risk!

The monthly expenses are based on real numbers in the Lease Option Refinance Strategy. Figure 3 shows the monthly cashflow numbers for the $350,000 property we're using in this example.

For these numbers, we have made various assumptions and naturally when you use this to determine the cashflow on your property, your numbers will be different. For example, here we are assuming a 3% mortgage rate, $400 in monthly property tax payments, and $150 in monthly insurance costs. The property management fee we're using here is $50, and we also want to earn a decent return for our trouble, so the occupant will be paying us simple interest at 12% per annum.

When we add up all those expenses, we obtain the monthly occupancy fee.

Monthly Cashflow			
Lease Payments		$2,684	$96,627
Less: Debt Service - 1st Mortgage	3.00%	($1,104)	($39,747)
Less: Investor return	12.00%	($980)	($35,280)
Less: Property Tax		($400)	($14,400)
Less: Insurance		(150)	($5,400)
Less: Property Management		($50)	($1,800)
Net		$0	

Figure 5-3: The Lease Option Monthly Cashflow

Most of the time, you will be estimating a lot of these numbers when you initially discuss this refinance strategy with the client and the broker, and therefore you may need to make some small adjustments as the numbers firm up and you get closer to the closing date. These changes can add to the paper burden, so it's best to get the best estimate possible when you're putting your numbers together. It should also be pointed out that I usually do the following when putting my numbers together:

- I use a mortgage rate for a fixed 3 year term in my cashflow estiamtes, even though I often stick with a 1 year fixed term.
- When estimating the monthly property taxes, I take the current tax amount and I add 10% to it because I am going to

assume that the property tax will increase at least 3% per year. The reason I do this is because I like to give the occupant a fixed monthly occupancy fee for full duration of the refinance term. This makes it very simple for everyone, but it also means that you will need to make these adjustments up front so that you don't end up losing out on anything if property tax rates increase.

Profit from Sale			
Sale Price (rounded to nearest $100)	2.25%	p.a.	$374,200
Less: Remaining 1st Mortgage			($245,504)
Less: Legal Cost to discharge			($1,500)
Less: Investor principal			($98,000)
Total Profit			**$29,196**
Total Returns for Investor			**$81,976**
Annualized Returns for Investor			**27.9%**

Figure 5-4: The Lease Option End of Term Profits

Finally, there are also expenses and profits to realize at the end of the 3 year refinance term, and these are shown in Figure 5-4.

One of the first things you will need to determine is the selling price of the property at the end of the 3 year term. This needs to be calculated upfront so the client can understand how much they will need to pay to get their home back. In this example, we are assuming a fairly conservative annual market appreciation of 2.25%, so the property that we paid $350,000 for will be sold back to the occupant in 3 years for $374,200. Next, we are going to assume there were no issues with the reserve fund, so the occupant's purchase option funds are returned to him. Since he is now becoming the buyer, he will use those funds as his down payment. If you did have to withdraw any funds from the reserve during the refinance term, then they would be subtracted from the tenant's total purchase option amount.

On closing, we also need to pay out the old first mortgage, and pay for our lawyer to close to the deal, and then we also need to pay ourselves back the initial amount that we invested in the property. Remember, this amount often comes from your home equity line of credit, so you are now paying off that outstanding debt.

When all is said and done on closing, you will have a profit of just over $29,000 for your efforts. When you add that profit to your monthly returns and upfront commission fee, you will realize an average annual return of 27.9%

A Typical Refinance Scenario: Make the Strategy Work in the Real World

There is a caveat here, however, and that is that since you borrowed your down payment and closing costs from your HELOC, you have had to make monthly interest payments during the term as well. These payments will reduce your actual profits somewhat and, when juxtaposed against expenses that you can write off against income from other sources, your true returns will depend on your particular financial circumstances. You may wish to discuss this further with your accountant.

Nevertheless, these are very healthy double-digit returns, and if you stick with the methodology and it's risk averse approach to investing, you could do very well following this.

As you can see, this is a very powerful real estate investment strategy. Even if you use it just once, you can realize returns that are only seen in riskier investments, except you don't take those crazy risks here! Of course, if you're looking to generate long-term wealth, then the thing to do is to take this process and do it over and over again with reinvested profits. That's the subject of our next chapter.

Chapter 5 Highlights

- Your profits and revenues are achieved up front, during and at the end of the refinance term.
- Expenses that the tenant pays as part of their monthly occupancy fee are based on real values – no magic numbers here.

Chapter 6

Turbocharge Your Wealth Through Lease Option Refinancing

*If you add a little to a little, and then do it again,
soon that little shall be much.*

Hesiod

One of the most important aspects of any investment plan is the ability to reproduce it any time, any where, and to be able to reinvest your profits in order to take full advantage of the compounding effect.

With this in mind, how do we use the Lease Option Refinance Strategy as the cornerstone of a much larger wealth-building methodology? Naturally, because the strategy can be used any time and virtually any where, the way to generate significant wealth is to take the profits from one transaction and reinvest them in more. This is an extremely powerful strategy for generating hundreds of thousands of dollars in a relatively short time – a decade or so – without taking on undue risk as long as you follow the steps closely, do your homework diligently, and keep your emotions in check.

It is worth stating again, however, that this is not a get rich quick scheme. If you follow the steps, you will generate wealth, but it will not happen overnight.

So let's take the very same process as we followed in the previous chapter, and take all our profits from the transaction and reinvest them once, twice, and three times to see what happens. This would mean that we're going to be operating on a 12 year horizon from the time of your first investment to the time you collect your profits on your last investments.

For the purpose of demonstration, let's assume that we're going to use all the same assumptions as before, so that we'll use the same mortgage rates, property taxes, annual market appreciations, and so on. With this in mind, when we look at the total profits from your first transaction – $81,976 – and add those to your initial line of credit amount of $98,000, we have a total investment pool of $179,976. That is, after the first Lease Option Refinance Strategy investment transaction, you will have about $180,000 to reinvest.

With this amount to invest, you will be able to purchase $642,771 worth of real estate. Now the chances are with this amount, you will likely be purchasing more than one property. That is, instead of buying a refinance property valued at $642,771, you will probably be looking at purchasing two properties valued at $321,385 or so. In other words, by following this strategy, you will be building your own real estate property portfolio.

Now the next thing to do is to use the same spreadsheets as before to determine your profits of this next round of lease option refinance investments. Once you have done that, we then determine how much cash you will have to invest once this new round is completed.

To save you the math, I have compiled these numbers, without rounding off, in the following figure 6-1.

Year	Investment Amount	Total Funds After 3 Year Terms
0	$98,000	$179,976
3	$179,976	$331,664
6	$331,664	$612,559
9	$612,559	$1,132,559
12	$1,132,559	$2,095,342

Figure 6-1: Lease Option Refinance Strategy applied over several years

There are some important considerations to keep in mind with the data in this table. For example, it does not account for the interest you pay on the amount you borrowed from your home equity line of credit. And, as we know, each situation is unique. But nevertheless, when you subtract your initial investment of $98,000 from this final amount and return that part to your HELOC, you are left with about $1,000,000 at the end of 9 years, and $2,000,000 at the end of 12 years.

What this means, of course, is that over a relatively short period of time, you will be build a significant amount of wealth. No more worrying about a pension plan... no more stress over the cost of sending your kids to college or university... no more wondering if you'll be able to afford that vacation. You will be able to have it all.

Without question, this is a powerful investment strategy that truly works, consistently, as long as you are disciplined in your approach and follow the low-risk philosophy outlined in this book. That said, there are no guarantees in life and this strategy is no exception. Your tenants' life situation may change, for example, and that could have a serious impact on your investment.

If you are using a professional management company or partnering with Cardinal Home Investments, you won't have to be as concerned with these changes compared to if you had to do it all yourself. Still, it's your investment so you will want to manage the process and stay on top of what's going on. With that in mind, in the next chapter, we're going to look at some of those situations where a tenant does not complete his refinance term and determine the impact of that on your investment.

Chapter 6 Highlights

- The key to turbocharging your wealth generation is to reinvest as much of the profits as you can afford. When you do this, you can achieve $1M in less than 10 years.
- Remember, this is not a get rich quick scheme. It takes time and effort but the rewards are huge – especially given the low-risk nature of lease option refinancing.

Chapter 7

When Your Investment Goes Horribly Wrong

Success is not final, failure is not fatal:

it is the courage to continue that counts.

Winston Churchill

In this chapter, I want to share with you two possible "disaster scenarios", and how we mitigate them to ensure that you as an investor do not lose any of your funds. But with that in mind, let me reiterate that investing in real estate is not for everyone. There are no guarantees in these types of transactions. The best thing for you to do is to get as much information about the process as possible. Check to make sure the financials on your lease option refinance property are solid and that you understand where all the numbers come from. Ask questions.

If you take your time reviewing potential investment opportunities and you follow the tenets of the Lease Option Refinance Strategy, you will greatly increase your chances of having a solid tenant who pays his monthly occupancy fee on time and goes on to complete the 3 year refinance term. That's the best possible scenario. However, there are times when life throws us a curve ball and no matter how well prepared we are, there remain some things that are out of our control.

It's impossible to forecast all disaster scenarios, but in this chapter, we're going to look at two situations that – should something go wrong – are the most likely we will ever encounter.

Disaster Scenario 1: The Tenant Gets Evicted

Let's take a look at what would happen if a tenant gets evicted. As far as we're concerned – and for the purpose of demonstration here – it doesn't matter why the tenant is evicted. We are most interested in how this impacts on our investment.

Using the same numbers and the same assumptions as we used in our Lease Option Refinance Strategy investment from earlier chapters in this book, we're going to start with a $98,000 investment in a $350,000 investment property. And we'll assume the same numbers as shown in the figures in chapter X.

Now let's assume everything's been going fine for the first several months but then the tenant's monthly occupancy cheque bounces. These things happen, so you immediately contact the tenant, indicating that his fee is due and there is also now a $200 penalty put on it. We'll assume your tenant has gone incommunicado, does not pay his monthly occupancy fee, and therefore you move quickly to evict him.

While he's being evicted, we will assume that he has not paid his monthly fee for 4 months. But during that time, you still have expenses to pay like mortgage payments, insurance and your own return. That's what the reserve fund is for, and since the tenant has forfeited his option payment credit (reserve fund), you must use those funds to cover off your monthly expenses.

So the situation is this. One year has passed since you made your purchase of the investment property. You have received monthly payments for 8 of those months. Three months' payments come from your reserve fund, and remember you have already collected "last month's payment", so you can use that too. The property is now empty and you estimate it will cost $500 to give it a good cleaning before you sell it. Remember, at this point your interest is simply to sell the home as quickly as possible, get your money out of it, and move on to another investment property. This is not the time to get greedy and try pushing the selling price. Find out what the market price is, price yours a bit lower, and sell the pig. The scenario is summarized in Figure 7-1.

Item	Expense	Proceeds	Balance
Market price @2.25% appreciation			$357,875
Reduced selling price			$353,000
Last Month's Rent		$2,684	$355,684
Reserve Fund		$32,209	$387,893
Cost to Prepare Property for resale	$500		$387,393
Cost of eviction - 3 months rent	$8,052		$379,341
Real Estate Sales commission 5%	$17,650		$361,691
Discharge 1st mortgage	$257,002		$104,689
Legal costs to sell property	$1,500		$103,189
Initial Investment	$98,000		$5,189

Figure 7-1: Disaster Scenario 1 – Tenant is evicted after 1 year

In the above disaster scenario, it is clear that even if you have to evict the tenant in the first year, and sell your property at a bit of a discount with the help of a real estate agent, you will still realize a profit of $5,189 when all is said and done. You could make even more if you have the time and skill to sell the property yourself.

Because you want to sell the property as quickly as possible, it is really important to follow the Lease Option Refinance Strategy investment parameters, like only purchasing good homes in good neighbourhoods in sound economic areas. This is so important for minimizing the time it will take to sell the property if you find yourself in this situation.

If you are using a property manager to undertake this work on your behalf, your expenses will be a bit higher too, and those will eat into your profit. However, even if you break even at the end of a year, you will still have recovered your initial investment of $98,000 plus you will have realized a 12% return on that too because you receive that return monthly, even if it comes from your reserve fund.

I often get the question: can this scenario happen in real life? The simple answer is yes. While the number of risk mitigation measures are considerable in the Lease Option Refinance Strategy, we have found that the first 6 – 12 months of life in the refinance term is the most challenging for tenants. They need to get used to managing their finances a different way. They need to start rebuilding their credit, which normally means doing things differently. These all factor into the process.

So the approach we take with the Lease Option Refinance Strategy is to *expect* that something will go wrong, and to be as prepared for that situation as best we can. Early eviction? Sure, we can handle that. We know what to do. And because of that, we can move quickly to evict tenants if needed and get the home on the market for resale. Now if you really don't have the skills to take this on, then you definitely should consider using a qualified and experience property manager to handle eviction matters on your behalf. This is not really something you can learn on the fly.

Let's now consider a different kind of scenario where the housing market actually drops in value over the 3 year refinance term. Because market volatility is something that seems to be the norm these days in many regions of the country, this is a particularly challenging scenario.

Disaster Scenario 2: The housing market drops over the refinance term

This particular scenario is a very real possibility and one that needs to be thought through carefully because no matter how well the program has worked, if the market drops significantly, then the tenant may simply walk away, leaving you with an over-valued property in a soft market.

As with the previous disaster scenario where the tenant gets evicted, the most important thing for you to do is to follow the rigorous risk mitigation approach of the Lease Option Refinance Strategy before you agree to accept someone. If it sounds like I'm a bit of a broken record on this point, it's only because it's so important. The better you select a tenant and property up front, the fewer problems you'll have later. So, **only accept carefully qualified clients and properties into the strategy**. Full stop. I can tell you, it is very tempting to tweak the qualification criteria in order to help out a single mom or a retired couple, even if the numbers aren't quite where they should be. But you do everyone a disservice if that happens. The Lease Option Refinance Strategy qualification criteria are strict and solid and proven. By following them, we significantly reduce the chances of potential disasters happening.

So to mitigate risk in the case of a market drop – which, by the way, we have no control over – we look for properties in economically sound areas and for tenants who have sufficient equity and income to be successful.

But despite the best research and the strictest criteria, life happens. Whether we have natural disasters or global conflicts or economic mismanagement, there are several events that can trigger a softening of the housing market that cannot be foreseen and are outside of our control.

So let's take a look at an example of a situation where the housing market drops 5% from the start of the refinance term to the end of it, and the tenant does not exercise his option to purchase. In other words, instead of overpaying for the property based on the agreed-to repurchase price, the tenant simply decides to walk away. Remember, as part of your Occupancy Agreement and Purchase Option Agreement with the tenant, he is obliged to purchase the property back from you for an agreed-to price, whether that price is higher or lower than market value. But since he has decided to walk away from the property in this situation, you now own a property that is worth less than what you paid for it three years ago.

Before we get too nervous about this situation, let's look at what you already have after three years, assuming the same property assumptions as we used earlier, that is, a $350,000 home. First, you have already collected your 12% per year returns, which equates to $35,280. Second, you have now collected the tenant's option purchase – the reserve fund – that is valued at $32,209. So in fact, you have already earned $67,489.

However, since the market has dropped 5% from the time you purchased the home, the value of the property now is only $332,500. So let's look at how the numbers shape up in Figure 7-2 below, and in this example, let's assume that it takes 2 extra months to sell the property.

Item	Expense	Proceeds	Balance
Market price @ 5% loss			$332,500
Selling Price of Property			$332,500
Reserve Fund		$32,209	$364,709
Cost to Prepare Property for resale	$500		$364,209
Time on market - 2 months	$5,368		$358,841
Real Estate Sales commission 5%	$16,625		$342,216
Discharge 1st mortgage	$244,514		$97,702
Legal costs to sell property	$1,500		$96,202
Initial Investment	$98,000		-$1,798

Figure 7-2: Disaster Scenario 2 – Housing market drops 5% over the refinance term

As shown in Figure 7-2, in this situation where the housing market has dropped 5% from the time you purchased the property, and if it takes you two extra months to sell it, it appears that you will lose about $1800. However, this does not account for the 12% per year returns you have already made, plus you have also earned another 2 months of returns while the property is being sold. That's an extra return of $1,960 which is actually more than you would lose. Again, you could save more money if you sold the home yourself or sold it sooner than 2 months on the market.

To summarize, even if your property loses 5% of its value over the refinance term, you still earn about 12% per year. That's still better than most investments out there.

The key to this is the face that the Lease Option Refinance Strategy demands at least 12 months of expenses as an option purchase credit, or reserve fund. Because of this, the chances of you actually losing any money are significantly reduced. That's why it's so important to follow the strategy and not get side-tracked by sad stories or suffering clients. Keep your emotions checked. Focus on the facts and the criteria in order to minimize your exposure to market fluctuations.

Some investors have asked whether they should actually hold on to the property, rent it out to someone else, and hold on to the property until the market recovers before selling it. That is certainly an option worth exploring if you are a hands-on investor or if you're comfortable with a property manager looking after those details. However, one thing you need to consider is whether the market rents will cover your expenses – including your 12% return – in order to make this option worthwhile. If you can make it work financially and are willing and prepared to do a little extra work as a landlord, then this is worth consideration. For most of us, we're not interested in the long term rental business. In my own personal case, although I still have a few long term rentals in my portfolio, my focus is on not on them: it's on the Lease Option Refinance Strategy.

There is a third scenario that many investors ask about, and although it's not exactly a disaster scenario, it is one that is of great importance to the tenant. Let's call it the...

Not-So-Disastrous Scenario 3: If the housing market drops 5%, can the tenant still purchase the property at the end of the term?

This is the same scenario as #2 except instead of walking away, the tenant wants to purchase the property back and is comfortable with his obligations for the agreed-to purchase price. Now the question that the tenant and his mortgage broker will be asking is: will I have enough of a down payment to purchase the home, given the change in its value? The reason why this is an issue is because he has agreed to pay more for the property than it is worth. A lender will only lend on the appraised value of a property, not necessarily what you paid for it. So that being the case, let's look at what might happen in this scenario. We'll use the same financials as we have throughout this book: an initial purchase price of $350,000 and so on. Please refer back to those numbers in Chapter 5.

From Chapter 5, the repurchase price was calculated to be $374,200 which is an average annual market increase of 2.25%. This is a conservative increase, as we discussed previously. But now we assume something has happened in the economy and the value of the property has dropped to $332,500. This means that the tenant is going to pay a lot more than what the property is worth; however, he's happy with that because it's his home and he wants it back, and plans to live there a long time so he feels he will recover his value in due course.

When the tenant goes to his mortgage broker for a new mortgage, he understands that the lender will only lend cash on the appraised value of the home, not on the purchase price. In many jurisdictions, you can purchase a home with very little down payment as long as you have some kind of mortgage insurance. In Canada, for example, you can purchase a home with 5% down. So let's go with that number and see what happens. The results are shown in Figure 7-3 below.

Item	Value
Market Price @ 5% loss	$332,500
Selling Price of Property	$374,200
Cash Required to Close	$58,325
Purchase Option (down payment)	$32,209
Value of First Mortgage @ 95%	$315,875
Shortfall	**$26,116**

Figure 7-3: Disaster Scenario 3 – Housing market drops 5% over the refinance term; can tenant still afford to repurchase?

As we can see from the numbers in Figure 7-3, if the market drops 5% from the time you purchased the property to the time the tenant needs to purchase it back, then there is a shortfall of just over

$26,000 and the tenant will need to find that extra cash in order to buy the property.

At this point, several things could happen. The first is, the tenant may decide that he can't afford to buy it back, and he can simply leave the property (see Scenario 2). The other thing that could happen is, if you choose, you could negotiate a new, lower repurchase price so that he can afford to buy the property back. You would not earn as much, of course, but at least you get the property out of your portfolio. A third thing that could happen is you could take that shortfall and put it into a second mortgage on the property. A fourth option is to extend the refinance term an additional year to see if the market picks up.

Depending on your comfort level and nature, you could choose any number of these options to help out the tenant; however, keep in mind that the tenant is obligated to pay the price that was agreed to, so it is within your rights to simply terminate the agreement if he is unable to close. That way, he forfeits his option payment and is forced to leave the home. You will still not make as much as you could have if the market had remained stable, but that is an option available to you.

The bottom line here is that no matter what the market does, you have a solid investment with minimized risk. No matter what may happen with the economy, the tenants or anything else, you have an exceptionally safe real estate investment that will serve you will.

Chapter Highlights

- As with any investment, there are no guarantees. So the best way to defend yourself against random events is planning for the worst.
- If, after you do your worst case scenarios, you do not think you can sleep at night, then this investment is not for you.
- Above all, remember not to panic. The reason why the rewards are so great with lease option refinancing is because there is some risk involved – no matter how well-mitigated. Don't panic… and just do what you need to do.

When Your Investment Goes Horribly Wrong

Chapter 8

How to Make Lease Option Refinancing Work With No Money of Your Own

The truth is you don't know what is going to happen tomorrow. Life is a crazy ride, and nothing is guaranteed.

Eminem

Everything so far in this book has been built around you, the investor, coming up with your own investment funds. This is accomplished either through your own cash reserves or a line of equity. But what if you don't have access to those funds? Perhaps you're a young adult who has only started working, with student loans to pay off and other expenses that most young people have. Is it still possible to take advantage of the Lease Option Refinance Strategy? Can you still start building your wealth now, or do you have to wait until you're in your middle years? Or, what if you don't have very good credit yourself?

I'm here to tell you that you can indeed start building your wealth without any funds of your own. That does not mean you can use some "no money down" scheme – this is not what the Lease Option Refinance Strategy is all about. You will need to find real investment funds.

Rather than go through a list of options with only marginal effectiveness – like holding a garage sale or finding a second job – let's cut right to the chase and focus on the one proven way to secure investment funds that has been used for centuries: finding a money partner.

The Money Partner

The money partner is going to provide you with all the cash you will need to invest in the Lease Option Refinance Strategy. This is going to be a joint venture partnership, which essentially means that while the money partner will provide the funds needed for investment, you will provide all of the strategic expertise and do all of the leg work. This will make it a true partnership.

Your Expertise + Partner Funds = A Solid Joint Venture

So in order to make this work, the onus is on you to become the most knowledgeable lease option expert around. You will need to know the strategy inside and out. You will need to build solid connections with mortgage brokers, lenders, real estate agents, and others involved in real estate investing. You should also join a local real estate investment organization in order to meet like-minded people. Just as an example, I offer weekend boot camps on the Lease Option Refinance Strategy where we go through all documents and scenarios in considerable detail. You can check the Cardinal Home Investments website at www.cardinalhomeinvestments.com or www.HootInvest.com for a schedule of these workshops. There is a lot to learn, but you can do it as long as you're willing to commit the time and energy to your training and learning.

To be clear, then, what you bring to the table in a joint venture partnership is the expertise. The money partner simply brings his cash. Together, you can use the Lease Option Refinance Strategy to generate considerable wealth.

Finding the Money Partners

Now let's consider where you can find these money partners. I can tell you from my own experience that there is no shortage of investment money out there, but there is a shortage of trustworthy partners and sound investment opportunities.

I hope that by now you are convinced that the Lease Option Refinance Strategy is a sound investment approach, especially when compared with other real estate deals or risky investment schemes that are out there. So your mission, should you choose to accept it, is two-fold: build your expertise in the Lease Option Refinance Strategy, and, in so doing, become a trustworthy investment partner. With this in mind, where do you find these money partners? There are essentially three places to look: your family, your circle of friends and associates, and then people you don't know.

There is no question that the best place to find a money partner is in your own family. Communities and successful businesses everywhere have been built on family money, and there's a reason why this is so. When family money is involved, the borrower is more likely to protect it. As well, family members tend to get more involved in the business opportunity, whether that's in the form of advice and guidance, or actual hands-on work.

In many communities, not only is family money available, but it is also expected that they will help each other out. But this is not always the case with others. For some, the idea of going to your dad or aunt or grandparents for investment funds can be awkward, totally uncomfortable, and frightening. This is where your newly-acquired expertise comes in to play. If you can demonstrate to your family that you know how the Lease Option Refinance Strategy works, and that you have already established a network of advisors and maybe even targeted some neighbourhoods for investment, then that will give you the confidence to present the strategy to potential money partners. By the way, this is true whether the partners are your family, friends, or total strangers. It is imperative that they see you as a credible expertise partner.

Family Members

Here are the steps you will need to take to explore potential partnerships with family members:

1. Prepare a Powerpoint presentation outlining the Lease Option Refinance Strategy. As one of my Platinum Members Investment Circle, you may use the free template for this available through your membership at www.HootInvest.com

2. Send the presentation to your family members and let them know about the lease option training you've taken and how you would like to work with them to generate wealth.

3. Prepare a plan for your investment strategy. You may not want to share this with your family right away, but it will come up at some point, so you'll need to have one ready. The thing is, when you're looking at the plan or discussing the strategy with any potential money investor, you need to be very clear – and make it very clear to them – just what exactly they are going to get out of the investment opportunity. Here are the things you should focus on:

a. potential returns, especially compared to their current returns;

b. relatively low-risk real estate investment – show them how the risks associated with real estate investment are mitigated using the Lease Option Refinance Strategy;

c. your plan on how you see the partnership working; that is, once the money partner has bought the property, how do you plan to manage it?

d. how you both benefit from the strategy and can use it to generate long-term wealth.

Without question, your best available source of funds is your own family. It costs you nothing to find them, and they are more likely to trust you with their funds than they would a complete stranger.

Friends and Associates

The next group you could approach is your circle of friends

and associates – those you work with or know from social activities. While this group may not know you as well as your family does, chances are good that because they at least know a bit about you and have a sense of who you are, they will be willing to listen to your plan for building wealth through the Lease Option Refinance Strategy.

Normally, the way you approach friends and associates is similar to the way you approach your own family. You will need to have a plan that illustrates your expertise and introduces the concept to them. You will need to have answers ready for all their questions (or at least know where to go to have them answered). So those steps that you put together for your family partners are the same you'll use for friends and associates too.

However, sometimes friends and associates also feel uncomfortable when someone approaches them about investment opportunities – especially if it seems like it's coming right out of the blue. When that happens, their shields go up and they have gone to yellow alert. As such, it's really important if not critical to take a low-key, non-sales approach with them. In other words, when you talk with them, you're not going to talk about investments or partnerships.

Say what?!?

Yes, that's true. You do not want to talk about partnering with them or building wealth together or any of that stuff because the goal of your meeting – whether that's over coffee or elsewhere – is about enjoying their company! So you talk about sports, or the kids, or going fishing or whatever it might be. The first and most important thing here is to remind them and yourself that you like them and that you appreciate their company.

But that doesn't mean you can't drop into the conversation something like the fact that you've been reading up on the Lease Option Refinance Strategy and that you find it pretty interesting. Or, that one of the things you're thinking about is investing in real estate. These allow you to gauge your friend's interest. If they start asking you questions about it, then you can follow up, but remember: this meeting is not about selling the concept; it's about appreciating your friendship.

If you're friend seems to be pretty interested in finding out more, then you can tell him that you're thinking of having a few friends over for an evening and that you'd be happy to go into more details about the strategy with them at that time. It will just be a small gathering of friends and associates where you can talk about investing strategies and where you'll share with them everything you've learned and what you have in mind.

This is the proven approach to finding potential money partners in your circle of friends and associates. It takes a little longer than it would with family members, and you may have to work a little harder to find them, but again because they know, like and trust you, they are usually willing to listen to your plan and give it some serious thought.

So here are the steps to take for finding money partners among your friends:

1. Make a list of all friends and associates who you like, and be sure to invite them out for a coffee just to catch up on the news of the world. Keep track of who has shown an interest in investing.
2. Invite a few of them over to your place, or another relaxed environment, for a fun evening where you can talk some more about investing and especially the Lease Option Refinance Strategy.
3. Prepare the same materials as you did for your family members.
4. Be sure to follow up with them a few days later to see if they have any interest in looking even more closely at the strategy and maybe even partnering with you to purchase an investment property.

Those are the basic steps to take. Remember, if your friends and associates start to think that they are somehow being ambushed into a sales pitch, they will drop you quickly and run for the door. This is only something that works with people you like and that you will hang around with irrespective of whether or not they eventually do end up investing with you.

Unknown Investors

The last group to go to are strangers. Here's the thing with strangers: there may be a lot more of them with a lot more cash to invest, but they are also harder to find, cost a lot more to find, and usually take a lot longer to get on board.

Let's think about why this is so. Suppose someone you had never heard of before and had never met came up to one day and said, "Can I partner with you to buy a $400,000 investment property?" What would you think about that? Exactly.

So, while there are more investors out there, finding them and convincing them of your own trustworthiness, along with the value of the strategy, can take a long time and can cost you a lot of money.

Nevertheless, sometimes you have no choice. So where do begin looking for these investors? They don't exactly advertise that they have money and that they're looking for investment opportunities, so where are they and, more importantly, how do you find them?

One way is to find them through independent financial advisors. A financial advisor typically has a list of clients they meet with and offer investment opportunities to. Their businesses are built on trust and performance. What they do is, when they introduce one of their investors to a product, they will earn a commission from the company offering that product. This fee varies from place to place, but can range from a few percentage points to 10% or more.

So, if you approached one of these independent financial advisors and showed them your Lease Option Refinance Strategy presentation, explained to them how their investors can benefit from partnering with you, then they may be interested in showing this to some of their clients. Their commission, by the way, is something that you would have to negotiate and build in to your financials. It means, in effect, that the investor will not make as much money (because the expenses are greater), but the returns should still be attractive.

You will face the same challenge with financial advisors as you would with an investor directly if they don't know you. However, if you focus on building a relationship with a financial advisor, then the hope is you'll be able to leverage their client base in order to build a list of possible investors. This will usually take a bit of time, so patience is the key for you. Your job here is, again, to know your strategy inside and out, and to be able to answer any questions that may get fired your way.

Chapter Highlights

- There is no shortage of investment money out there. The challenge has always been to find it and attract it to you.
- The way to attract investment funds is to become an expert in the 7-Step Lease Option Refinance Strategy. You will be the real estate expert, and then you will be able to convince investors that you are solid, reliable, and able to make the strategy work.
- Be sure to let everyone you know that you are looking for investment funds to invest in real estate lease option refinancing. Go on all the social media sites and let the world know what exactly you are looking for. Then follow up with your expertise.

Chapter 9

Frequently Asked Questions on Lease Option Refinancing

A wise man can learn more from a foolish question than a fool can learn from a wise answer.

Bruce Lee

When you start discussing the 7-Step Lease Option Refinance Strategy with others—whether that's mortgage brokers, bankers or homeowners—you will get a lot of questions. This is not a strategy that everyone knows about, so part of your job as the lease option expert is to inform others as best as you can so they can make good decisions.

In this chapter, we're simply going to go through a lot of questions and answers that I've had to deal with over the years. Some of these questions are really basic, but some are quite complex. In order to demonstrate your credibility and build trust with your team and homeowners, you will need to understand the system extremely well and one of the best ways to do this is to review these FAQs often and to start keeping your own.

How much investment money do I need to get started?

This will depend on where you intend to invest, since the housing market varies by region and by neighbourhood. As a rule of thumb, I don't invest in anything under $200,000 in my area where the current average price of a single-family home is $350,000. If you take $200,000 to the minimum in which you will invest, then you will need about $56,000.

How long is my investment tied up?

In the Lease Option Refinance Strategy, the typical term length is 3 years. If you go less than that, then you won't realize as many profits when you sell the property back to the tenant since it won't have as long to grow. If you go longer than 3 years, then the risk increases because there's more of a chance that something could go wrong. So I always stick with 3 year terms.

Who actually owns the investment property?

You do. If you join up with a money partner, then the money partner is usually the only one on title, unless you are also putting in funds towards the purchase.

Can I use the Lease Option Refinance Strategy with registered funds like an RRSP?

Unfortunately, no. Registered funds cannot be used to purchase an investment property. You will need to find cash.

If I own an investment property using the Lease Option Refinance Strategy, can I sell it to someone else before the term is up?

No. The tenant has the first right of refusal when you sell. That's what he's paying for when he provides you with an option payment.

What happens if the tenant cannot buy the property back after the refinance term?

Two things can happen. First, if the tenant is almost ready and able to purchase the property back but just needs a bit more time (usually determined in consultation with a mortgage broker), then you may both agree to extend the Occupancy Agreement by up to 12 months, under the same terms and conditions. However, if the tenant is unable to purchase the property back, then he is forced to leave at the end of the Occupancy Agreement, and he forfeits his option payment credit.

Who actually controls the tenant's purchase option funds?

According to the Purchase Option Agreement, you receive these funds on closing from the tenant. However, I recommend that you not simply put these funds into your private bank account. Instead, you should leave them with your lawyer in trust, and draw down on them only if you need them to cover off a missing rent payment from your tenant. As well, the funds should be placed in a joint bank account by your lawyer that includes the tenant's name on it. While the tenant will not be able to withdraw these funds, the mortgage lender will see that these funds will be returned to the tenant if they successfully complete the refinance conditions.

What happens if the market value of the property drops?

If the value of the property drops over the course of the refinance term, the tenant is still obligated to pay you the price that you agreed upon up front at the start of the lease. Thus, if the value of the home is $200,000 at the end of the term, and you have agreed with the tenant up front that the repurchase price will be $220,000 then he can only purchase the home back at that price.

Conversely, if the market increases more than expected, you cannot increase the repurchase price. So if the value at the end of the term is $250,000 and you agreed that the repurchase price would be $220,000 then the tenant is in fact buying the home back at below market value.

Where do I find lease option refinance clients?

You should not have much difficulty finding qualified clients for this strategy. Your network of mortgage brokers is your best source, so be sure to make yourself known to them. You can also find them through kijiji or other on line notice boards. As well, you can email me personally to see my inventory.

Should I invest in condos?

No. They are way too risky. Heed the words of the Jedi Council, Padawan! Just say no.

Does the Lease Option Refinance Strategy work for farms or vacant land?

Sort of. Let me explain. The Lease Option Refinance Strategy outlined in this book is designed for single family homes only. However, you can use a lease option strategy like this one – with various modifications – if you so desire. Now having said that, I would never use lease option refinancing on cottages, farms, vacant land, mobile homes or condos or anything other than a nice suburban home. I don't like the risk.

What does the mortgage broker do?

The mortgage broker does two jobs. First, she often identifies the potential tenant for you since that's where homeowners go when they cannot get their existing mortgages renewed. So she will be able to send clients your way. As part of this, she will also collect all of the documents that you'll need for your due diligence and qualification process.

The second thing she does is work with the tenant so they can repair their credit and position themselves to secure a new mortgage at the end of the lease option refinance term.

Do you provide advisory services in case I need some help or more information?

Yes! I often work with investors to provide advice and guidance and support services to them as part of my ongoing commitment to this strategy. Investors working with me also have the benefit of the expertise of my team at Cardinal.

Can I partner with someone else to use the Lease Option Refinance Strategy?

You must certainly can! And, in fact, this is how many would-be investors begin generating their own wealth when they're just starting out. See Chapter 8 for more information about how to do this.

If I'm a homeowner and I need refinancing, how do I find someone to do the lease option refinance for my home?

You could check with your local mortgage broker, or come directly to Cardinal. We also work with homeowners and help bring them together with investors looking for investment opportunities. More information on this program is available on the website at www.cardinalhomeinvestments.com

How do I make money with the Lease Option Refinance Strategy?

As an investor, you make money three ways with the Lease Option Refinance Strategy. First, you make an up front 5% commission when you purchase the investment property. Then, you make a monthly return of 12% per annum during the 3 year term. Finally, you also make a profit when you sell the property back to the tenant at the end of the refinance term. There is no waiting around for your returns to realize under the Lease Option Refinance Strategy…you are always earning something.

What happens if the tenant abandons the property before completing the refinance term?

This is a possibility and is covered in detail in Chapter 7, but the bottom line is this: if the tenant abandons the property part way through, then not only do you the property you can sell, but you also keep the tenant's option payment which is worth tens of thousands of dollars.

Can I use the Lease Option Refinance Strategy anywhere in North America?

Each jurisdiction is different, so you will have to look closely at your own, but generally wherever you can lease a car with an option to buy, you can also use the Lease Option Refinance Strategy because the basic concept of the lease option – someone paying you an option payment for the first right of refusal to repurchase their home – is the same.

If, for some reason, your jurisdiction frowns upon lease options as they relate to real estate investments, you can still invest using the Lease Option Refinance Strategy elsewhere in North America where there aren't as many challenges. Contact me at david@cardinalhomeinvestments.com or david@hootinvest.com

Chapter 10

The Cardinal Home Investments Refinance Program For Investors

It is not only one person's work, it's really a partnership and collaboration during all these years.

Christo

I've mentioned Cardinal Home Investments a few times in this book, and if you will indulge me for a short period of time, I'd like to show you what Cardinal does. If you're the kind of investor who doesn't want to get involved in the day-to-day management of an investment portfolio, then this chapter will be of particular interest to you.

Cardinal is an Ottawa-based company that works directly with investors and homeowners. We provide a full range of real estate

investment services, including:
- valuable information and strategies for investors
- consulting and advisory services
- property management services
- mortgage broker networking
- brokering services (bringing investors and homeowner clients together)
- credit counseling
- training

While many investors who learn about the Lease Option Refinance Strategy prefer to take a hands-on approach, the vast majority are not interested in the day-to-day operational work of managing tenants, dealing with municipalities, following up on property management needs, evictions (if needed) and so on. This is where a company like Cardinal, with a solid track record, becomes a critical partner in your wealth-building strategy.

Cardinal has a small, professional management team along with a nation-wide network of highly skilled associates. No matter where you are, or where you want to invest, we can help you get there.

Glossary of Terms

Keeping track of all the terms used in this strategy and in real estate investing generally can be challenging some times. I've brought all of the most important terms together in this glossary so you have a place where you can find just about anything.

Annualized Rate of Return
The annualized rate of return is taking the entire profit from an investment, determining the return on investment, and dividing it be the number of years that you invested your money. For example, if your total return on an investment was 60%, and you held your investment for three years, the annualized rate of return would be 60% / 3 years = 20% per year.

Credit Score
This is a statistically-derived numerical summary of the information contained in your credit report. It indicates your credit worthiness for a lender.

Credit Report
A detailed report of an individual's credit history, usually compiled by a credit bureau. It shows whether the individual pays his bills on time, including credit cards, loans, taxes, mortgages and so on.

Due Diligence
The care that a reasonable person takes when evaluating an investment opportunity.

Equity
This is the value of a property that remains after all debts associated with the property have been paid out. It is the difference between the property value and the property debts.

Eviction

This is the process that will remove negligent tenants from your income generating property. It is not an easy process and you may wish to rely on the services of an experienced property manager or eviction specialist to get deadbeats out of your property so you can sell it.

Home Equity Line of Credit (HELOC)

A home equity line of credit is a type of revolving fund, like a credit card, that is secured by the value of your home. It is usually maxed out at 80% of your home's value. The HELOC is calculated by taking the appraised value of your home, multiplying by 80%, and then subtracting the outstanding mortgage debt. The remainder represents the line of credit from which you can borrow funds. The key benefit of the HELOC is that you only pay interest when you use the funds, and the interest rate charged is usually considerably lower than a conventional bank loan.

Lease Option

This is a process in which the Lessor pays to the Lessee a "consideration" for the option to do something at the end of the term. For example, with the Lease Option Refinance Strategy, the Lessor (tenant) will pay to the Lessee (the investor) a consideration for the right of first refusal to purchase the home back after a specified length of time and for a specified price.

Lease Option Agreement

This is the contractual agreement that sets out the terms and conditions of the lease option arrangement. It is legally binding.

Letter of Direction

A letter of direction is a one page document that the tenant will give to their lawyer in order to close the deal and enter into the lease option refinance arrangement. In our scenario, the tenant—prior to closing—will send a letter of direction to her lawyer stating that different amounts of the proceeds of sale will be sent to various parties. These parties include the investor and debt holders. The letter of direction is a critical component of the Lease Option Refinance Strategy. As an investor, you will not close a purchase deal unless there is a letter of direction showing where the proceeds will be going.

Mortgage
A loan given to a property owner in which the loan is legally secured by the asset.

First Mortgage
This is the first loan provided by a lender on a property. It is in first position, which means that when the property is sold or otherwise disposed of, this is the loan that gets repaid first.

Second Mortgage
This is a second loan given to the owner of the property and is secured by the asset itself. When the property is sold or otherwise disposed of, this loan gets paid out second, after the first mortgage is paid out.

Occupant
This is another term used for a tenant, and refers to the person who is actually living in the home.

Occupancy Agreement
The occupancy agreement is like a lease between a renter and a landlord. It stipulates the terms and conditions of the arrangement between the investor (landlord) and the renter (occupant). While not exactly a rental agreement, it is often considered to be the same thing.

Option Payment Credit
This is the amount of money that the occupant pays you, when you purchase his property, for the right to purchase the home back at the end of the lease option refinance term. It also serves as security for you since, if the occupant defaults on his agreements, he forfeits this amount. In the Lease Option Refinance Strategy, the option payment credit is at least 12 months worth of expenses.

Per annum (PA)
This simply means "per year". So a 12% per annum return means you will receive 12% per year.

Property Management Agreement

This is the contract that you will sign with a property management company if you choose to take a hands-off approach to managing the tenants during the term of the Lease Option Refinance Strategy. It stipulates what you will pay for the various services that you require.

Purchase and Sale Agreement
This is the agreement you use to purchase the property from the tenant. Different jurisdictions have different pro forma agreements that you can use Check with your local real estate association for these forms.

Purchase Option Agreement
The purchase option agreement specifies the repurchase price of the property at the end of the lease option refinance term. Again, like the lease option agreement, it stipulates various terms and conditions.

Return on Investment (ROI)
The ROI is calculated by taking all of the profits that you made on an investment, and dividing it by how much you initially invested. For example, if you invest $20,000 and your profits total $5,000 then your ROI is $5,000 / $20,000 = 25%

Tenant
A tenant is someone who occupies a property he doesn't own, and pays rent on a monthly basis to the owner of the property for its use (the landlord). In the Lease Option Refinance Strategy, the tenant is also known as the occupant.

Total Debt Service Ratio (TDSR)
The TDSR is defined by taking the sum of your annual mortgage payments PLUS your property tax PLUS any other annual debt payments and dividing that sum by your gross family income. Typically, if this ratio is 40% or lower, banks will see you as a good bet for being able to service your mortgage. However, that ratio can vary because some lenders will accept a higher limit and others will only accept a lower value.

Appendices

MS-Word files of these agreement templates are available to all my Platinum Members Investment Circle who sign up for a minimum three months. Membership cost is only $19.95 per month or $199.95 per year at www.HootInvest.com/InvestmentCircle.html. Go online or see page 158 for more details.

These templates are for illustrative purposes only. No warranty is made to their completeness or suitability for individual use. Consult a lawyer prior to executing any legal document.

OCCUPANCY AGREEMENT

This agreement is made between:

Investor
(hereinafter referred to as the "Owner")

and

[Occupant Name]
(hereinafter referred to as the "Occupant")

Whereas the Occupant agrees to enter into this Occupancy Agreement (the "Agreement") for the property located in the City of [   ], in the Province of [   ], and municipally described as [   ] (hereinafter the "Premises");

1. The Owner grants to the Occupant and the Occupant accepts from the Owner, upon the terms and conditions contained herein, the Premises.

2. The term hereof shall commence on [   ] (the "Commencement Date") and continue for a period of [12] months (the "Term"). Provided the Occupant is in good standing, the Term shall automatically renew for a further [12] months on the day before the anniversary of the Commencement Date to a maximum Term of [36] months (the "Option Purchase Date")

3. The Occupant shall enter into a purchase option agreement (the "Option Agreement") and shall have the right to purchase the Premises according to the terms and conditions in the Option Agreement. If the Occupant does not exercise

its rights pursuant to the Option Agreement, the Occupant shall vacate the Premises at the end of the Term.

Initials: _____   Initials: _____
   Owner   Occupant

4. The Occupant(s) shall pay as a monthly Occupancy Fee (the "Occupancy Fee") the sum
of [CDN$ X,XXX.XX]. The Occupancy Fee shall be payable in advance, on or before the [ ] of each calendar month (the "Due Date"), as directed by the Owner from time to time. The Occupancy Fee may be mailed using Canada Post / USPS at the Occupant's sole risk. Any Occupancy Fees that are not received by the Due Date or are lost in the mail are treated as if unpaid. Any Occupancy Fees that are received after the Due Date shall be in the following priority: first applied toward collection costs, including any and all legal fees, second applied towards Occupancy Fees in arrears, and third the monthly Occupancy Fee.

5. The Occupant shall pay to the Owner the amount of [$] which shall represent the amount of first and last month's Occupancy Fees.

6. An additional service charge of $200.00 shall be paid to the Owner for all dishonoured or "non sufficient fund" ("NSF") cheques or for late payment of any reason. If the Occupants Occupancy Fees are NSF, the Owner reserves the right to demand certified cheques or money orders or automatic bank-to-bank payments on all future payments. If any Provincial monthly payment control laws do not allow the above procedure or any procedure contained in this Agreement, the Provincial laws will prevail. The Occupant agrees to provide an Equifax credit report every twelve (12) months from the Commencement Date through the Term, if requested by the Owner.

7. In the event of late payment of Occupancy Fees, the Owner shall have the right to deduct such fees from the occupant's option payment credit, as per the Option Agreement.

8. In the event that the Occupancy Fee is not received within five (5) days of the Due Date, the Occupant(s) is considered to be in default of the Agreement and Option Agreement as per the default provisions in section 19 below.

9. The Premises shall be used as a residence with no more than [ ] adult and [ ] children whose names are as follows:

_____
_____
_____
_____

The Premises shall not be used for any other purpose without the prior

Appendices

written consent of the Owner.

10. The Occupant shall pay all utilities and services for the Premises (eg. hydro, gas, water, garbage collection, telephone, television, internet, etc.) in a timely manner. The Occupant agrees to have the electricity, natural gas, and water held in his/her name as of the Commencement Date. Upon request by the Owner, the Occupant shall provide proof of timely payment of such utilities and services.

11. With respect to pets on the Premises, no pets are permitted without the prior written consent of the Owner. As of the date of this Agreement, the following pets shall be kept on the Premises: _____.

12. The Occupant agrees not to assign this Agreement, nor to sublet any portion or the property, nor to allow any other person to live therein other than persons named above without first obtaining written permission from the Owner. The Occupant will be responsible for all administrative costs incurred by the Owner. Further, it is agreed that covenants contained in this Agreement, once breached, cannot afterward be performed and that legal proceedings may be commenced at once, without notice to the Occupant, (other than any notice required by Provincial laws).

13. The Occupant acknowledges that the Premises are in good order and repair, unless otherwise indicated herein, and accepts same in "as is" condition. Furthermore:

    (a) The Occupant shall, at their own expense, maintain the Premises in a clean and sanitary manner and in good condition including all equipment, appliances, furniture and furnishings therein and shall the surrender the same at the conclusion of the Term, except for normal wear and tear.

(b) The Owner may at any time give the Occupant a written inventory of furniture and furnishings on the
    Premises and the Occupant shall be deemed to have possession of all said furniture and furnishings in good condition and repair, unless he objects thereto in writing within 5 days after receipts of such inventory.

(c) The Occupant shall water and maintain any surrounding grounds, including lawns and shrubbery, and keep the same clear of rubbish and weeds when such grounds are part of the Premises and are for the exclusive use of the Occupant.

(d) The Occupant may paint, wallpaper or otherwise redecorate or make alterations to the Premises with the prior written consent of the Owner.

(e) All costs for any redecorating or alterations shall be paid 100% by the Occupant and no consideration by the Owner will be made to the Occupant for any said work.

(f) Any major or structural changes must be approved in writing by the Owner and shall only be completed with proper permits and by qualified professionals.

(g) Should this Agreement be cancelled for any reason, there will be no credit or consideration returned for repairs, alterations or decorations.

14. In addition, the Occupant shall be responsible for all repairs, maintenance costs, and service charges including but not limited to: furnace, air conditioning, roof, plugged toilets, sinks and drains, replacing all broken windows and screens, employees, contractors, invitees, guests, replacing light bulbs, fluorescent tubes, stove fuses, broken toilet seats, and any other damaged items. The Occupant agrees to immediately report to the Owner any and all damage that may occur to the Premises and or property by way of, not limited to: accident, breakage or defect throughout the continuance of this Agreement. In the event the Occupant fails to complete maintenance/repairs, the Owner shall have the option to complete the necessary work and deduct any and all incurred fees from the occupant's option payment credit.

15. The Owner and Occupant agree that the Owner holds the right to inspect the Premises at the Commencement Date and at the end of the Term, and that the condition of the Premises at the aforesaid times will be noted on an inspection report (the "Inspection Report") which shall form part of this Agreement. Both the Owner and the Occupant with sign the Inspection Report. The Owner shall use the Inspection Report as proof of the condition of the Premises at the time of the inspection and for determining damages and for seeking appropriate deductions or compensation from the Occupants. The Owner reserves the right to take photographs at both aforesaid times for further documentation to the condition of the Premises.

16. The Occupant agrees it is the responsibility of the Occupant to insure the Occupant's property on the Premises against damage or loss of such property occasioned by fire, theft and any other perils. The Occupant's policy shall waive all rights of subrogation against the Owner and its servants, agents and contractors.

17. The Occupant hereby waives and releases the Owner from any liability whatsoever for damage or loss to any persons or property whatsoever which occurs in or in connection with the Premises and any improvements, building or property thereon or from the Occupant's use of the premises however caused, including loss due to negligence or fault of the Owner and its servants, agents or contractors (Occupant to look to its own insurance and insurers for recovery of and protection against any such loss or damage). Without limiting the generality of the foregoing, the Owner shall not be responsible for any loss of Occupant's property in the premises or stored in, at or near the building due to any cause whatsoever. Occupant shall on demand provide a copy of insurance to the Owner

18. In the event that the Premises is damaged by fire and through no fault of the

Appendices

Occupant and cannot be restored within a reasonable time at the sole and unfettered discretion of the Owner, this Agreement shall terminate with no further liability of either party and all remaining monies returned to the Occupant.

19. The failure of the Occupant to make any and all necessary payments under this Agreement, or to perform any of the terms or conditions in this Agreement shall be considered a default. In the event that the Occupant shall be absent from the Premises for a period of five (5) consecutive days while in default under this Agreement, the Occupant shall at the option of the Owner, be deemed to have abandoned the Premises and any personal property left on the Premises shall be considered abandoned and may be disposed of by the Owner in any manner allowed by law. In the event that the Owner reasonably believes that such abandoned property has no value, it may be discarded. All property on the Premises is hereby subject to a lien in favour of the Owner, for payment of all sums due hereunder, to the maximum extent allowed by law. Recovery of the Premises by the Owner shall not relieve the Occupants of any obligations hereunder, and the Owner may lease the Premises to others upon such terms and conditions they deem proper, and recover the Occupant sums due hereunder, less any consideration received from others for the use of the Premises, for the remaining term hereof, after paying any and all expenses.

20. The acceptance by Owner of partial payments of monthly Occupancy Fees shall not, under any circumstances, constitute a waiver of Owner, nor affect any notice or legal proceedings therefore given or commenced under Provincial law. If the Occupant defaults on any other provisions under this Agreement, including but not limited to, any misrepresentation on the Occupant's application, the Owner in their sole discretion, can elect to continue this Agreement or terminate this Agreement and take possession of the Premises by any legal means available. The Owner is not required to give any notice to cure a violation of this Agreement, other than what is required by law.

21. All rights given to the Owner by this Agreement shall be cumulative to any other laws, which might exist or come into being. Any failure of the Owner to enforce any of the provisions or restrictions herein contained shall in no way be deemed a waiver of the right to do so thereafter or insist upon strict compliance of the terms hereof. No statement or promise of the Owner, servants or their agent as to tenancy, repairs, alterations, or other terms and conditions shall be binding unless reduced to writing and signed by the Owner.

22. Should any provisions of this Agreement be found to be invalid or unenforceable, the remainder of the Agreement shall not be affected thereby and each term and provision herein shall be valid and enforceable to the fullest extent permitted by law.

23. The Owner has the right of emergency access to the Premises at any time and access during reasonable hours to inspect the property or show it to prospective Occupants with a 24 hour notice to Occupant. The Owner shall retain a key at all

times. If the Occupant wishes to change the locks, the Occupant must notify the Owner in writing and provide a new key immediately. The Owner shall be entitled to view and inspect the property upon reasonable notice to the Occupants, at least twice a year, on or about the first day of spring and the first day of fall to check the batteries in the smoke detectors throughout the property.

24. Occupants shall comply with all municipal, provincial, and federal laws, statutes, and ordinances now in effect, or which shall be enacted in the future, and any violation of such shall be a complete and material breach of the lease.

25. Occupant agrees without protest to reimburse the Owner for all actual and reasonable expenses incurred by way of Occupant's violation of any term or provisions of this lease, including but not limited to a $50.00 fee for each notice, Notice to Quit, or other notices mailed or delivered by the Owner to Occupant due to Occupant's non-payment of Occupancy Fee or other breach of lease, all court costs and including costs of a solicitor and his own client full indemnity basis , and all collection costs. Any such costs are due immediately as additional Occupancy Fee. Any payments received by the Owner will be applied first towards late fees and/or other additional charges, then toward the Occupancy Fee. Both the Owner and Occupant waive trial by jury and agree to submit to the personal jurisdiction and venue of a court of subject matter whose jurisdiction is located in the area in which the property is located. In such event, no action shall be entertained by said court or any other court of competent jurisdiction, if filed more than one (1) year subsequent to the date the cause(s) of action accrued. In the event that the Owner shall prevail in any legal action brought by either party to enforce the terms hereof or relating to the demised Premises, the Owner shall be entitled to all costs incurred in connection with such action, including legal fees of a solicitor and his own client, full indemnity basis. The Owner is entitled to recover an allowance for his time and effort expended with respect to any default recovery proceedings at the rate of $50.00 per hour. Such allowance is deemed to be reasonable and comparable with what the Owner would pay to a third party for a similar time and effort.

26. Occupant hereby waives any and all rights to assert affirmative defenses or counterclaims in any eviction action instituted by The Owner with the exception of an affirmative defense based upon payment of all amounts claimed by the Owner not to have been paid by the Occupant.

27. If the Owner is unable to deliver possession of the premises at the Commencement Date, the Owner shall not be liable for any damage caused thereby, not shall this Agreement be voided or voidable but Occupant shall not be liable for any payment of Occupancy Fees until possession is delivered. If possession cannot be delivered within fifteen (15) days from the Commencement Date, this Agreement shall be null and void at the sole option of the Owner and all deposit monies returned to the Occupant. In the alternative, the Owner may extend the commencement date of the Agreement for a period of up to thirty (30) days, from the expiry of the aforesaid fifteen (15) day period but if possession cannot be

delivered to the Occupant within the aforesaid thirty (30) day period, the within Agreement shall be null and void and all deposit monies returned to the Occupant.

28. This agreement shall constitute the full and complete understanding of the parties and supersedes all prior written or oral agreements. There shall be no further additions or changes to this agreement unless the same is reduced to writing and signed by both parties.

29. Any notice which either party may or is required to give, may be given by mailing the same, postage
prepaid, to the Occupant at the Premises or to the Owner at the address shown below or at such other places as may be designated by the parties from time to time:

To Owner: _____
_____
_____

30. Owner hereby advises Occupant that by signing this Occupancy Agreement, Occupant is entering into a legally binding agreement with Owner. Owner recommends and advises the Occupant to obtain independent legal advice regarding the terms of this agreement prior to signing this agreement. Occupant acknowledges and agrees that sufficient opportunity has been given to obtain independent legal advice. Occupant further acknowledges and agrees that such independent legal advice has been obtained;

31. THE OWNER ASSUMES NO FINANCIAL RESPONSIBILITY FOR ANY ECONOMIC LOSS ASSOCIATED, AND NOT LIMITED TO, EXPENSES OR LOSSES ARISING FROM THE PARTIES ASSOCIATED WITH THIS AGREEMENT. THE OWNER INDEMNIFIES ITESELF, OWNERS AND AGENTS FROM AND AGAINST, AND NOT LIMITED TO ALL CLAIMS, DEMANDS, LOSSES, EXPENSES, DAMAGES, ACTIONS, SUITS AND OTHER LEGAL PROCEEDINGS, JUDGMENTS, SETTLEMENTS OR ANY OTHER MATTER SIMILAR OR DISSIMILAR IN ANYWAY ARISING FROM, BY REASON OF, IN CONNECTION WITH OR BASED UPON, INCLUDING COSTS AND EXPENSES ARISING OUT OF ANY NEGLIGENT ACT OR OMISSION OCCASIONED BY OR OTHERWISE ATTRIBUTABLE TO THE OCCUPANT OR OWNER ASSOCIATED WITH THIS AGREEMENT.

Initials: _____   Initials: _____
       Owner   Occupant

32. This Agreement is binding upon and inures to the benefit of the heirs, assigns

and successors in interest to the parties.

[THE REMAINDER OF THIS PAGE LEFT INTENTIONALLY BLANK]

33. The undersigned Occupant hereby accepts and understands all terms of this Agreement, including all schedules, and acknowledge receipt of a copy hereof.

IN WITNESS WHEREOF the Parties have hereto affixed their hands and seals or their corporate seals attested by the hands of their duly authorized officers, as of the Date of Agreement.

_____
Per: Investor Name

_____   _____
Witness: Occupant:

_____   _____
Witness: Occupant:

Appendices

PURCHASE OPTION AGREEMENT

This Option to Purchase dated this [   ] day of [   ], 20xx between:

Investor
(hereinafter referred to as the "Optionor")

and

[Occupant(s) Name]
(hereinafter referred to as the "Optionee")

WHEREAS the Optionee has entered into an Occupancy Agreement (the "Occupancy Agreement") with the Optionor for the property located in the City of [   ], in the Province of [   ], and municipally described as [   ] (hereinafter the "Premises");

1. In consideration of the sum of one ($1.00) dollar paid by the Optionee to the Optionor, and so long as the Optionee is not in default of the Occupancy Agreement or this Purchase Option Agreement (the "Agreement"), the Optionee shall have the option to purchase the Premises described herein (the "Option"), in accordance with this Agreement.

2. The option purchase price for the Premises shall be [$XXX,XXX.XX] (hereinafter, the "Purchase Price").

3. The Optionee shall have paid the sum of [$ XX,XXX.XX] as a non-refundable option payment credit (the "Option Payment Credit") . The Option Payment credit shall be applied as a credit to the Purchase Price on closing only if the Optionee exercise their rights under this Agreement. IN THE EVENT THAT THE OPTIONEE FAILS TO EXERCISE THIS AGREEMENT OR DEFAULT UNDER ANY TERM OF THIS AGREEMENT OR THE OCCUPANCY AGREEMENT, THIS AGREEMENT SHALL BE NULL AND VOID AND ALL MONIES HELD BY THE OPTIONOR SHALL BE RETAINED BY THE OPTIONOR AS LIQUIDATED DAMAGES AND NOT AS A PENALTY.

Initials: _____   Initials: _____
      Owner   Occupant

4. The Option Payment Credit shall be paid directly to the Owner for their absolute and immediate unfettered use and benefit. Interest accrued on the original Option Payment Credit amount, along with the Option Payment Credit itself, shall

be applied as a credit at closing in accordance with section 9 below.

5. The Option may be exercised at any time after twenty-four (24) months from the Date of Commencement as defined in the Occupancy Agreement, and shall expire forty-five (45) days before the last day of the Occupancy Agreement, unless exercised prior thereto. Upon expiration, the Owner shall be released from all obligations hereunder and all the Occupant's rights hereunder, legal or equitable, shall cease.

6. The Option may be exercised at any time after a minimum of twenty-four (24) months has passed. The Optionee will be responsible for providing the Expiration of Option Fee, along with any additional fees or penalties incurred by the Owner for breaking his mortgage obligations early, and a fifteen hundred ($1,500.00) dollar administrative fee.

7. The Option shall be exercised by mailing or personally delivering written notice to the Owner sixty (60) days prior to the Expiration of the Option and by additional payment, on account of the purchase price, in the amount of [$X,XXX.XX] (the 'Exercise of Option Fee") payable directly to the Owner.

8. Notice, if mailed, shall be registered mail, to the Owner at the address set forth below and shall be deemed to have been given upon the day following the day shown on the post office receipt:

To the Owner: _____

_____

_____

9. In the event that the Option is exercised, the Option Payment Credit shall be a credit toward the Purchase Price. The Option Payment Credit will only be credited if the Option is exercised and the transaction is completed. IF THE OPTION IS NOT EXERCISED OR THE OPTIONEE IS IN DEFAULT OF THE OCCUPANCY AGREEMENT OR THIS AGREEMENT, THE OCCUPANT FORFEITS THE OPTION PAYMENT CREDIT.

Initials: _____   Initials: _____
      Owner   Occupant

10. By exercising the Option, the Optionee agrees that the obligation to purchase is unconditional and creates a binding Agreement of Purchase and Sale between Optionee and Optionor. The Optionee will complete any and all necessary paperwork to that effect. The Optionee also acknowledges they will be responsible for paying any and all provincial Land Transfer Taxes that may be due on registration of the transaction.

11. Upon payment of five hundred ($500.00) dollars, the Optionee shall

have the right to extend this Option by twelve (12) months under the same terms and conditions of this Agreement.

12. The completion date of the purchase shall be sixty (60) days from the date of exercise of the Option or such other date as the parties may agree upon.

13. This Option, or any interest therein, is not transferable or assignable and the Option can only be exercised by the individuals signing this Agreement.

14. The Optionee agrees and understands that a fundamental condition of this Agreement is that all terms and conditions of both this Agreement and the Occupancy Agreement must not be in default, or expired, or this Agreement t will be null and void.

15. To further clarify, all covenants of said Occupancy Agreement and this Agreement must have been faithfully performed in order for this Option to be valid and enforceable. This includes, but is not limited to, the repairs, maintenance and upkeep of said property, payment or other obligations required under this Agreement or Occupancy Agreement. Default of any of the terms and conditions of this Agreement or Occupancy Agreement shall result in this Option being automatically null and void and any monies paid hereunder retained by Optionor as liquidated damages and not as a penalty.

16. The undersigned Optionee acknowledges that they have read this Agreement, understand it, agree to it and have been given a copy. They further have been advised to seek legal, tax, technical expertise and any other counsel of their choosing concerning this contract and prior to signing. The Optionee acknowledges and agrees that you have been given sufficient opportunity to obtain independent legal advice and further acknowledge and agree that you have obtained such independent legal advice as you consider necessary and advisable.

17. There shall be no further additions or changes to this agreement unless the same is reduced to writing and signed by all parties.

18. The Optionee shall comply with all municipal, provincial, and federal laws, statutes, and ordinances now in effect, or which shall be enacted in the future, and any violation of such shall be a complete and material breach of this Agreement. The Optionee have no authority to, and shall not cause any lien to be placed against the subject legal title.

19. This Agreement, including any schedules attached hereto, constitutes the entire agreement between the parties pertaining to the subject matter of this Agreement and supersedes all prior agreements, understandings, negotiations and discussions, whether oral or written, of the parties. There are no representations, warranties or other agreements, whether oral or written, between the parties in connection with the subject matter of this Agreement except as specifically set out in this Agreement.

20. All references to the Optionee herein employed shall be construed to include the plural as well as the singular, and the masculine shall include the feminine and neuter where the context of this Agreement may require.

21. If any section or portion of this Agreement is determined to be unenforceable or invalid for any reason whatsoever that unenforceability or invalidity shall not affect the enforceability or validity of the remaining portions of this Agreement and such unenforceable and invalid section or portion thereof shall be severed from the remainder of this Agreement.

22. The failure of either party to enforce any provision of this Agreement will not be construed as a waiver or limitation of that party's right to subsequently enforce and compel strict compliance with every provision of this Agreement.

23. This Agreement shall be construed in accordance with and governed by the laws of the Province of Ontario, except as to its principles of conflicts of law.

IN WITNESS WHEREOF the parties have hereto affixed their hands and seals or their corporate seals attested by
the hands of their duly authorized officers, as of the date of this Agreement.

_____
Per: Investor's Name

_____   _____
Witness: Optionee:

_____   _____
Witness: Optionee:

About The Author

David Hamilton is a real estate investor, teacher and writer. He is President of HootInvest.com – an Ottawa-based online company that specializes in providing advice, tools and information to assist investors with achieving their real estate goals, especially using the 7-Step Lease Option Refinance Strategy. He is also CEO of Cardinal Home Investments, a company that brings investors together with homeowner clients who need refinancing and cannot get it through traditional methods. David is married and lives in Ottawa, Ontario. He and his wife Susan have one son, Spencer.

Become a Platinum Member in David Hamilton's HootInvest.com Investment Circle!

To become a Platinum Member in David Hamilton's HootInvest.com Investment Circle and receive numerous free downloadable templates, member-only articles, personal email connection and coaching with David Hamilton, valuable insider information, discounts on products, and member-only investment opportunities, just go online to:

www.HootInvest.com/InvestmentCircle.html

and fill in the online form to get started. Payment is made through PayPal, so you can use debit or credit card. The cost to become a Platinum Member is only:

$19.95 per month (3 month minimum)

Or

$199.95 per year (savings of $39.45 annually)

Introducing…

The 7-Step Lease Option Refinance Strategy Home Study Course

If you like what you see in this book and want the benefit of a more detailed, step-by-step home study course with personalized coaching, then this is the home study course for you. And you can pre-order it right now at a special discount.

Here's what you'll get:
- The 7-Step Lease Option Refinance Strategy Home Study binder
- Lease option contract and agreement templates that you can use right away
- The Financial Analyzer excel spreadsheet to help you understand your investment opportunities
- David Hamilton's personal Property and Tenant Evaluation Scorecards
- over 7 hours of audio training covering each of the 7 Steps
- Free subscription to David Hamilton's newsletter *Real Estate Investing the Low-Risk Way*
- Free one year Platinum Membership in David Hamilton's HootInvest.com Investment Circle
- up to 2 hours of personal coaching with David Hamilton
- How to invest $50,000 in a lease option home and receive over $8,900 on closing.

But that's not all. I'll also include for you:
- Bonus powerpoint presentation you can use to find investment partners
- two fully-detailed case studies that you can follow, showing you exactly how the lease option refinance strategy works.
- Bonus audio on "How I am Using the 7-Step Lease Option Refinance Strategy to Build Millions"

Total Value: $1,497.00
Pre-Order Special: $997.00

100% Money Back Guarantee

If for any reason you are not entirely satisfied, you may return all the resources from the 7-Step Lease Option Refinance Strategy anytime within 30 days of receipt, and receive a full no-questions-asked refund.

This is a **limited time offer** and once the home study course is available, this special pre-order price will no longer be offered.

Take action now!

Go to www.HoctInvest.com/7stepcourse.html to pre-order your very own 7-Step Lease Option Refinance Strategy Home Study Course and get it delivered to your home before anyone else receives it. Payment is made through PayPal, so you can use debit or credit card.